DIRECTIONS IN DEVELOPMENT

Assessing Student Learning in Africa

DIRECTIONS IN DEVELOPMENT

Assessing Student Learning in Africa

Thomas Kellaghan and Vincent Greaney

THE WORLD BANK
Washington, D.C.

© 2004 The International Bank for Reconstruction and Development/THE WORLD BANK
1818 H Street, NW
Washington, DC 20433 USA

Telephone   202-473-1000
Internet   www.worldbank.org
E-mail   feedback@worldbank.org

All rights reserved
First printing

1 2 3 4 07 06 05 04

Cover photos by (clockwise from upper right) Michael Foley, Ami Vitale, and Eric Miller.

ISBN 0-8213-5849-9

Library of Congress Cataloging-in-Publication Data has been applied for.

Contents

Acknowledgments

The authors wish to acknowledge the assistance of the following in the preparation of this paper: Tunde Adekola, R. Agabu, Jean-Marc Bernard, E. D. Bononewe, Jaap Bregman, Vinaygum Chinapah, Paul Coustère, Brigitte Duces, Mourad Ezzine, Birger Fredriksen, Jacques Hallak, Soumana Hamidou, Cathal Higgins, Anil Kanjee, John Khozi, John Lauglo, Meskerem Mulatu, Paud Murphy, Bob Prouty, Rachidi B. Radji, Ken Ross, Wendy Rynee, Charlotte Sedel, Endale Shewangizaw, Mercy Tembon, Gary Theisen, Adriaan Verspoor, and David Weere. Secretarial assistance was provided by Hilary Walshe.

Abbreviations

ADEA	Association for Development of Education in Africa
ARB	Assessment Resource Bank
DAE	Donors to African Education (now the ADEA)
EFA	Education For All
EMIS	Educational Management Information System
ERGESE	Evaluative Research of the General Education System in Ethiopia
IEA	International Association for the Evaluation of Educational Achievement
IIEP	International Institute for Educational Planning
LWC	Language of wider communication
MDGs	Millennium Development Goals
MLA	Monitoring Learning Achievement
MOE	Ministry of Education
NESIS	National Education Statistical Information Systems
PASEC	*Programme d'Analyse des Systèmes Educatifs des Pays de la CONFEMEN*
PIRLS	Progress in International Literacy Study
PRSPs	Poverty Reduction Strategy Papers
SACMEQ	Southern Africa Consortium for Educational Quality
SAP	Structural Adjustment Program
TIMSS	Third International Mathematics and Science Study
UNESCO	United Nations Educational, Scientific and Cultural Organisation
UNICEF	United Nations Children's Fund
WGES	Working Group on Education Statistics
WGSE	Working Group on School Examinations

Executive Summary

The World Bank policy paper of January 1988, *Education in Sub-Saharan Africa, Policies for Adjustment, Revitalization, and Expansion* (World Bank 1988), placed a major focus on improving academic standards through the reform of examination systems. In June 1988, Donors to African Education (now the Association for the Development of Education in Africa, ADEA) signalled its interest in examinations when it set up a Working Group on School Examinations to study and promote the role of examinations in quality improvement. Following this, the World Bank Education and Training Division of the Africa Technical Department prepared terms of reference for studies of examinations in primary and secondary education in Sub-Saharan Africa. The studies were carried out with funding from the World Bank and the Irish Government in six Anglophone countries, six Francophone countries, and two other countries. A report on these studies, *Using Examinations to Improve Education: A Study in Fourteen African Countries*, was prepared by the authors of the present paper and was published by the World Bank in 1992 (Kellaghan and Greaney 1992).

This paper reviews what has happened in the field of assessment since then. It deals with public examinations, but differs from the 1992 report in that, other than in regard to a few minor details, no new data were specifically collected for it. The paper revisits many of the issues that were raised in the earlier report, particularly in relation to the role that assessment can play in improving the quality of students' learning. It also differs from the earlier report in that its consideration of assessment is not limited to public examinations.

The World Declaration on Education for All in Jomtien in 1990 not only gave fresh impetus to issues relating to assessment, but also necessitated the introduction of a new form of assessment—system assessment, or national assessment—to determine if children were acquiring the useful knowledge, reasoning ability, skills, and values that schools promised to deliver. National assessment is the second major area of assessment addressed in this paper. International assessments, which share many procedural features with national assessment, are also considered. The fourth type of assessment addressed in the paper is classroom assessment.

Public Examinations

Public (external) examinations have played a major role throughout the history of modern education in Africa. They serve a number of functions, the most important of which is to select students for successive levels in the education system. They have, however, repeatedly been criticized for their quality. In particular, it has been observed that examinations are limited in the areas of knowledge and skills that they assess; they contain little reference to the knowledge and skills that students need in their everyday life outside school; and they tend to measure achievement at a low taxonomic level.

This situation has two implications. First, there are questions concerning the validity of the examinations. In particular, because they are biased toward the testing of competencies needed by the minority of students who will continue their education into the next cycle, they do not adequately reflect the goals that the curriculum sets for those students who will not proceed. Second, when external examinations have important consequences related to performance, serious concerns arise about their effect on the character and quality of teaching and learning.

Several education systems have over the past two decades taken steps to improve the quality of examinations by, for example, using more diverse modes of assessment, by including items that test higher-order thinking skills, and by assessing the ability of students to apply their knowledge and skills in situations outside school as well as in a scholastic context. The expectation is that such improvements will influence what is taught and what is learned. To reinforce the impact of examinations on practice in schools, some countries also have put in place a number of additional procedures. These include the publication of examination results (to increase competition between schools), the provision of information on student performance, the provision of support and guidance to underperforming schools, and the establishment of linkages between examinations authorities and those responsible for curriculum development and implementation.

Efforts to improve the quality of examinations are to be commended and encouraged, but one should hesitate before placing too great a reliance on the ability of examinations to alter the quality of learning for all students. While changes in the content areas examined can change the content to which students are exposed in class, there is limited empirical evidence that they will produce an improvement in the overall level of student achievements or in the cognitive processing skills of students. The fact also that high stakes are attached to examination performance can have a number of negative, if unintended, consequences for school practice, whatever the quality of the examinations. These include a narrowing of the areas of the curriculum that are taught and an associated neglect of what is not examined; an emphasis on learning strategies that are superficial or short-term (such as memorizing, rehearsing, and rote learning); the devotion of a significant amount of time to test-preparation activities; and a heavy reliance on extrinsic rather than intrinsic motivation in student learning. Of particular significance in the context of Education for All is the fact that teachers, because their reputations depend on how well their students perform in examinations, may focus their efforts on those students who are most likely to succeed. This may be associated with high rates of grade retention and early dropout.

National Assessment

While public examinations are a long-standing feature of education systems, national assessments (sometimes called system assessments, learning assessments, or, less appropriately, assessments of learning outcomes) are relatively new. A national assessment may be defined as an exercise designed to describe the level of achievement, not of individual students, but of a whole education system or a clearly defined part of one (such as grade 4 pupils or 11-year-olds). National assessments were introduced to address the fact that the educational data on inputs to education that typically had been collected in the past were often of little relevance or use to educational planners. National assessments would address this issue by providing information on the "products" or "outcomes" of schooling (such as student achievements or inequalities in the system). This information, it was hoped, could be used in conjunction with input data to provide a sounder basis for policy- and decision-making in education.

Five main issues are addressed in national assessments: How well are students learning? Is there evidence of particular strengths or weaknesses in their knowledge and skills? Do achievements of subgroups in the population differ? To what extent is achievement associated with characteristics of the learning environment? And do the achievements of students change over time?

During the 1990s there was a great deal of activity in Africa relating to national assessment. Four major categories of this activity can be identified. Three involve similar activities in several countries: the Monitoring Learning Achievement (MLA) project, the Southern Africa Consortium for Monitoring Educational Quality (SACMEQ) project, and the *Programme d'Analyse des Systèmes Educatifs des Pays de la CONFEMEN* (PASEC). To date, MLA assessments have been carried out in 47 countries in Africa, SACMEQ assessments in 15, and PASEC in 9. The fourth category comprises national assessments, unrelated to any of these activities, that were carried out in individual countries.

All of the assessments share a number of common features. All are policy-oriented, involving planners and managers, and are designed to provide information for policymaking. All assess student achievements in basic curriculum areas. All are sample-based. All view capacity building and the strengthening of the policy/research nexus as major objectives. And all use an input–output model of the education system and attempt to identify factors associated with achievement.

The assessment programs have achieved reported impact in policy debate and formulation, in reviews of educational policy, in national education sector studies, in reappraisal of the adequacy of resources, and in supporting policy decisions. Several countries have operated as many as three national assessments, each sponsored or supported by a different agency. This would suggest that the assessments were not a response to locally perceived needs and that they are not integrated into the normal structures and activities of ministries. Given the need for such integration, the cost of these activities, and problems in recruiting personnel with the required competence to carry them out, it is clear that there is an urgent need for rationalization.

International Assessments

International assessments differ from national assessments in that they can provide some indication of where the achievements of students in a country stand relative to the achievements of students in other countries. They also provide evidence on the extent to which the treatment of common curriculum areas differs across countries.

Only a few African countries have participated in international assessments, but the MLA, PASEC, and SACMEQ projects, while designed as national assessments, also permit international comparison.

Classroom Assessment

The assessment of student learning in the classroom, as conducted both by teachers and by students, is an integral component of the teaching–learning process. Much of this kind of assessment is subjective, informal, immediate, ongoing, and intuitive, as it interacts with learning as it occurs, monitoring student behavior, scholastic performance, and responsiveness to instruction. Its role is to determine an individual student's level of knowledge, skill, or understanding; to diagnose problems that he or she may be encountering; to assist in making decisions about the next instructional steps to take (that is, to revise or to move on); and to evaluate the learning that has taken place in a lesson.

There is evidence that the quality of teachers' assessment practices may be deficient in many ways. Problems that have been identified include the use of poorly focused questions, a predominance of questions that require short answers involving factual knowledge, the evocation of responses that require repetition rather than reflection, and a lack of procedures designed to develop students' higher-order cognitive skills.

With some notable exceptions in Francophone countries, the improvement of classroom assessment has received little attention in reforms. Given its central role in the teaching–learning process, such improvement should be accorded high priority in any reform that has as its objective the improvement of student learning.

Several examination systems in Africa have introduced or are planning to introduce an element of school-based assessment in their public examinations. Some hope ultimately to replace external examining with school-based assessment, especially at the primary school level, perceiving this to be the only way in which the range of competencies specified in the curriculum can be validly assessed and in which the negative effects of external examinations can be removed. The implementation of school-based assessment as a component of public examinations has proven problematic, however. While the aspiration and motivation to introduce it have been high, practical difficulties have on more than one occasion resulted in its failure, postponement, or limitation to a minimal amount.

Using Assessment and Examinations Information in the Classroom

Getting information to teachers and effecting changes in teacher behavior is not easy. Expectations that information from assessments and examinations can radically alter the culture of schools and substantially raise the achievements of all students are unrealistic. There are numerous factors that can frustrate the intentions of reformers, and unless these are recognized and addressed, the impact on the quality of student learning of policies involving assessment may be limited. These constraining factors include the following: the mode of intervention, relevance of information, teacher competence, teacher understanding of the implications of changes, the complexity of teaching, the classroom context, and opposition by teachers and parents based on the perception that change will involve a risk to their children.

Mechanisms to Support the Use of Assessment

While assessment information can improve policy and the management of resources in education and shape the instructional practice of teachers, the use of assessment data does not guarantee success. Success in the first place is dependent on the political will of the government to support the effort. At one level, national assessment systems should be institutionalized and integrated into the structures and processes of government policymaking and decision-making. This will require national assessment to be aligned with other major instructional guidance systems of the education system, along with other assessment systems (including the alignment of standards), curricula, teacher education, school capacity building, and measures to address inequities. Action is also required at the school level, and includes the opening of adequate channels of communication in which teachers are informed about the implications of assessment findings. This can be difficult when problems relate to instructional objectives, equity, and quality. Teachers may need considerable and continuing support to help them interpret reforms and to devise appropriate teaching strategies based on their interpretations.

1

The Context of Proposals to Use Assessment to Improve the Quality of Education

The 1990 World Conference on Education for All (EFA) in Jomtien, Thailand, held out the promise of improving the equity and quality of education systems worldwide as nations sought to secure their economic competitiveness in a globalizing economy. Not only would education be open to all children, but those who would avail themselves of the opportunity for learning would acquire useful knowledge, reasoning ability, skills, and values (UNESCO 1990).

Since the conference, student achievement has become a major point of reference in judging the quality of education. Because the conference recommendations represented the convergent views of national governments, organizations, and donor agencies, they have had enormous influence. Countries throughout the world have responded by giving priority to basic education, promoting gender equity in access to education, improving opportunities of rural and the poorest population groups, improving quality at all levels, addressing the issue of the practical relevance of school curricula, and capacity building.

The aspirations of the conference were in many respects not new. From the 1960s to the 1980s, many developing countries had proposed programs that sought to achieve the quantitative expansion and qualitative improvement of primary education. The goals of these programs included the establishment of a better balance between academic and practical/technical subjects; the integration of school and community activities; the improvement of teacher preparation; the extension of inspection, supervision, and advisory services for teachers; improvements in the methods of assessing pupils; the increased availability of textbooks; and enhancement of the efficiency of educational planning (Grisay and Mählck 1991). The Jomtien declaration differed from these earlier programs through having an international and interagency dimension; but, significantly, it also required definitions of or targets for quality improvement and specified the need to assess the effects of reforms on student achievements.

1

Extent and Quality of Educational Provision in Africa

It is easy in retrospect to say that the target of the Declaration on Education for All—to ensure that all nations would have universal basic education by 2000—was overambitious. It was not met. Some countries forged ahead, others sustained their gains without making any new breakthrough, and others slipped backward (S. Nalovu, cited in ADEA 1999). In Sub-Saharan Africa, while net enrolment increased, post-1980 the nonenrolled school-age population also increased (this following a decrease in the 1970s) (UNESCO 2000a). An estimated 42.4 million school-age children in Africa do not attend school (UNESCO 2002).

Getting all children into school is only a first step in achieving the goal of education for all, however. Reform must focus on learning acquisition and outcomes, rather than merely on enrolment. The magnitude of this task becomes clear when one considers the quality of education provided for those who do attend school. At a regional conference on EFA for Sub-Saharan Africa, held in Johannesburg in December 1999 and attended by ministers of education and representatives of civil society and international development agencies, it was concluded that the education provided was "poor and the curricula often irrelevant to the needs of the learners and of social, cultural and economic development" (UNESCO 2000b, p. 26); that "education planning and management capacity … remain largely underdeveloped" (p. 26); and that "only a small proportion of children are reaching the minimum required competencies and our education systems are not performing to the standards we expect of them" (p. 28).

Observation of education in individual countries across the continent reinforces this gloomy picture. The poor quality of education in Ghana, for example, is underscored by "abysmal national criterion-referenced test scores" from 1992 through 1996 (N'tchougan-Sonou 2001). In Ethiopia in 1990, more than 20 percent of candidates failed the grade six examination, 40 percent failed grade eight, and 70 percent failed the senior secondary leaving examination. This was so despite a high retention rate in schools. In Mozambique, one-third of grade five pupils and one-half of grade seven pupils did not pass the national examinations (Takala 1998). In Senegal between 1990 and 1995, the average success rate in the end of primary school examination was less than 30 percent (ADEA 2002). And in Guinea, in tests that were constructed to reflect the objectives of the curriculum, only 6 percent of pupils achieved "mastery" in French. None achieved mastery in mathematics (Carron and Châu 1996).

Obstacles to Meeting EFA Goals

The effort to implement the policies of EFA unfortunately came at a time when many countries on the continent were suffering from civil strife, natural disasters, and the HIV/AIDS pandemic. They also occurred alongside the implementation of Structural Adjustment Programs (SAPs), which made expenditure on education vulnerable. SAPs typically aimed to increase efficiency (by reducing unit costs) and cost recovery (by raising fees and encouraging private provision) in secondary-level education, measures that in conjunction with the drive to increase the provision of education were unlikely to improve quality. However, "ultimately, whether or not education contributes to development depends less on how many children complete school than on what they do or do not learn" (Samoff 1999, p. 199).

Given the lack of human and financial resources to carry out the EFA mandate, it was to be expected that the enormous expansion of education that has taken place in Africa would be accompanied by a deterioration in quality (see Bude 1993). Uganda, for example, had little hope of maintaining, much less improving, quality when primary school enrolment was rising from 2.5 million (in 1996) to 6.5 million (in 1999) and the pupil–teacher ratio was declining from 38:1 to 62:1 (ADEA 1999). In Zambia, the Focus on Learning task force noted in a follow-up to Jomtien that the "price that has been paid for the rapid quantitative developments of earlier years is a serious deterioration in the quality of school education" (cited in Takala 1998). Many countries appear to have given little consideration to the inevitable effect on quality of a policy that stressed quantitative expansion. Parents, however, did notice, questioning the value of education for their children as quality dropped sharply, less-qualified teachers were employed, classes became larger, facilities deteriorated, and textbooks fell into short supply (Chapman and Mählck 1993).

Recommitment in Dakar to EFA

Progress during the 1990s can only be regarded as disappointing. In 2000, national governments, organizations, and donor agencies recommitted themselves to EFA with the Dakar Framework for Action (UNESCO 2000a). A revised set of goals was set that included:

- ensuring that by 2015, all children, particularly girls, children in difficult circumstances, and those belonging to ethnic minorities, have access to and complete primary education of good quality (goal 3);
- eliminating gender disparities in primary and secondary education by 2005 and achieving gender equality in education by 2015, with a focus on ensuring girls' full and equal access to and achievement in basic education of good quality (goal 5); and
- improving all aspects of the quality of education and ensuring excellence of all so that recognized and measurable learning outcomes are

achieved by all, especially in literacy, numeracy, and essential life skills (goal 6) (UNESCO 2002, p. 13).

Unlike the Jomtien Declaration, the Dakar Framework specified a set of actions that were designed to instil a sense of urgency and create a climate of accountability (UNESCO 2002). The policies and practices adopted in pursuit of EFA goals will depend on local circumstances and thus will vary from country to country, but since all countries are committed to recognized and measurable learning outcomes, some form of assessment will be required to determine if these are achieved.

The need to assess student achievements will require departure from the practice in which the focus when assessing the quality of education typically has been on inputs, such as student participation rates, physical facilities, curriculum materials, books, and teacher training (Grisay and Mählck 1991). Inputs have some relevance in an assessment of quality, but the assumption is not always tenable that high-quality inputs are associated with high levels of student achievement. By the same token, what are often considered low-quality inputs are not always associated with low levels of achievement.

The growth in interest in ascertaining what students learn at school is not attributable solely to a commitment to monitor the effect of EFA policies, nor is it confined to developing countries. In recent years, interest in developing a corporatist approach to administration has become evident in both the industrialized and developing worlds, as has an associated rise in "managerialism." This corporatist approach draws on ideas from the business world that include strategic and operational planning, continuous improvement, a focus on "deliverables" and results, quality assurance, incentive and accountability systems based on results, and the concept of the citizen as consumer. Above all, it defines performance in terms of results: Performance targets are set, the extent to which results are achieved is determined on the basis of performance indicators, and decisions regarding resource allocation are based on the results achieved. The primary purpose of these activities is to provide rapid and continuous feedback on a limited number of outcome measures considered to be of interest to politicians, policymakers, administrators, and stakeholders (Kellaghan 2003; Kellaghan and Madaus 2000).

Focus of the Paper

This paper focuses on the use of assessment to monitor and evaluate learning. Acceptance that there is a need to monitor what students learn gives rise to four specific needs (UNESCO 2000b):

- the need to describe the knowledge and skills that constitute "quality education;"

- the need for the technical means and organization capacity to measure student achievement;
- the need for the technical means to evaluate progress toward the goal of "quality education;" and
- the need for expertise in translating assessment data into policy and instructional procedures that will improve the quality of learning.

The term "assessment" will be used to refer to any procedure or activity that is designed to collect information about the knowledge, attitudes, or skills of a learner or group of learners (Kellaghan and Greaney 2001b). Four major categories of assessment will be considered: public (external) examinations, national assessments, international assessments, and classroom assessment. It should be noted that each category comprises a variety of practices. The categorization, is justified, however, on the basis that administrative procedures vary for the categories and the major purposes of assessment in the four categories differ.

On the basis that government response to problems in the past was constrained by the fact that little objective information on which to make decisions was available to managers, we shall be interested as we consider each category in determining the extent to which information derived from assessments can help decision-makers improve the management of and, in turn, the quality of the education system (see Chapman and Mählck 1993). The use of information derived from assessments may not be limited to management decisions: When performance assessment has important consequences (as is the case when performance on a public examination determines graduation, promotion, or selection for further education or a job), it is likely to directly impact on teaching and learning. As such, it merits consideration as a mechanism by which to improve student achievements.

In the context of EFA, the main interest in assessment has been in monitoring the outcomes of the education system rather than in appraising the achievements of individual students. This interest is addressed in our description of national and international assessments. However, given the important role that the assessment of individual students in public (external) examinations plays in the education systems of Africa, we also consider how examinations might be used to shape teachers' pedagogical practices in desirable ways, and thus to improve the quality of student learning.

Classroom-based assessment has received little attention in proposals for the use of assessment to improve student learning. This may be because it is difficult for policymakers, over a short period of time or without getting involved in what is likely to be expensive in-service provision, to influence the classroom practices of teachers. From the perspective of changing teaching practices, it may be easier and less expensive to use an existing, centrally controlled system of assessment (public examinations) or to mandate an external assessment (in a national assessment) than to rely on in-service training. The assessment by teachers of student learning in the classroom occupies a central role in the learning process of all students, however, and as such should be taken into account when formulating proposals to improve learning through the use of assessment.

2
Public (External) Examinations

Public (external) examinations have played a major role throughout the history of modern education in Africa. In most countries, three major examinations are administered by an agency outside the school (in Anglophone countries, usually a national examinations authority, and in Francophone countries the ministry of education). The first examination is administered at the end of primary schooling, when students are tested in the major subjects of the curriculum (typically English or French, a local language, science, and social studies). Performance on the examination usually determines whether or not a student will proceed to secondary school. After two or three years in secondary school, students sit the second examination (usually in a wider range of subjects), the results of which determine who moves on to the higher grades of secondary education. At the end of secondary school, a third public examination is administered, the results of which affect the student's further educational and vocational prospects.

The central importance of public examinations in Africa can be attributed to the fact that they serve a number of functions that reflect the social and educational contexts in which they are administered. First, by specifying clear goals and standards for teachers and students, they control the disparate elements of the education system, helping to ensure that all schools teach to the same standards. This was particularly necessary in colonial times, when most schools were privately managed. Second, public examinations are perceived to allocate scarce educational benefits in an objective and unbiased way (although there are concerns that they may discriminate against minorities, rural populations, girls, and students whose first language differs from that of the examination). Third, the examinations have a certification function. This function tends to be overlooked because of the emphasis placed on the use of examination results to inform selection for continuing education, but formal certification of academic achievement can help students to gain access to employment or training. (It should be noted, however, that lower-level certificates are losing their currency in the labor market as the numbers possessing them increase.) Fourth, examinations can be used to underpin changes in curriculum and teaching methods, and to maintain national standards. Fifth, examinations may serve an accountability function for teachers and schools. This is especially the case where the results of student performance on examinations are published. Finally—and especially at the end of secondary schooling—examinations legitimate membership in the global society and facilitate international mobility (Kellaghan 1992; Kellaghan and Greaney 1992; Omolewa and Kellaghan 2003).

This section considers first the quality of public examinations in Africa. While over the past two decades, many countries have striven to improve the quality of their examination systems, many examinations nonetheless are inadequate. Some of the demonstrated inadequacies are inherent in any terminal pencil-and-paper test, but even given this format, improvements could be made. Following a description of the quality of examinations, we describe how data from examinations can provide insights into the nature of student achievements at the end of a course of study (for example, by helping identify curriculum areas in which students perform poorly), and how it can be used to describe how those achievements are distributed by gender, by school, and by region. We then consider the rationale behind proposals to use examinations as a lever of reform, and review the limited empirical evidence relating to the effects of changes in examinations on what is taught in classrooms and on student achievements. We also describe a number of mechanisms that are designed to use assessment data to bring about change in school practice and pupil achievements. Following a consideration of the problems that arise when high-stakes examinations are used to influence teaching and learning, we propose a number of guidelines to improve the quality of examinations.

It should be noted that our commentary relates to the formal education system. This should not be taken to imply that the nonformal sector is an unimportant component of educational endeavor in Africa. There are, for example, many cases of students in this sector being prepared for public examinations, and in many systems, there are also large numbers of "external" candidates who do not attend recognized schools. (These often are students who have underperformed in an earlier sitting of an examination; they would be likely to attend courses that generally are regarded as falling within the nonformal sector.) That public examinations are not generally considered relevant to nonformal education is due largely to differences in the goals of formal and nonformal education, differences in the characteristics of the participants in the two sectors, and a reluctance on the part of many nonformal educators to get involved in the formal assessment of student achievements. Given that some participants in nonformal education may wish to enter the formal sector, however, arrangements should be put in place to establish equivalences between the qualifications obtainable in the two sectors.

The Quality of Public Examinations in Africa

Studies and official reports have identified numerous inadequacies in examinations which have important consequences attached to performance. Principal among these are the following (ERGESE 1986; Kellaghan and Greaney 1992; Kelly 1991; Little 1982; Oxenham 1983; Somerset 1996):

- Most examinations at primary and secondary level are limited to pencil-and-paper tests. As such they ignore a variety of areas of knowledge and skill, often specified in curricula, that cannot be measured by such tests.
- Examinations, particularly in languages and mathematics at the end of primary schooling, emphasize the achievement of cognitive skills and pay very little attention to practical skills.
- There is evidence that items in many examinations measure achievement at a low taxonomic level (involving the recall or recognition of factual knowledge), rather than measuring the skills students will need in later life, such as the ability to synthesize material or apply knowledge to new situations (for example, in making inferences, developing a logical sequence of steps to solve a problem, or arguing a case).
- Many examinations make little reference to the everyday life of students outside school. They deal for the most part with scholastic topics and applications, rather than, for example, trying to establish if a student can use money in the marketplace or can deal with health problems in the home.
- The quality of questions in examinations is often poor: questions may be poorly phrased, the alternatives in multiple-choice tests may be unsatisfactory, and scoring criteria may lack clarity.

There are two major implications of this situation. First, it brings into question the validity of the examinations. In particular, there are concerns about the extent to which they are biased toward the testing of competencies needed by students in the next cycle of education. Do the examinations adequately reflect the goals of the curricula for those students (a majority in most countries) who will not proceed further in the education system? Second, since teachers focus their teaching on what is likely to be assessed in a "high-stakes" examination, serious concerns have been raised about the character and quality of teaching and learning in schools.

Improving the Quality of Public Examinations

The countries of Sub-Saharan Africa have over the years made many attempts to improve the quality of their examinations. The changes often have been technical, designed to improve efficiency. For example, as student numbers have grown, the task of processing examination scripts also has grown. Many countries have responded by adopting a multiple-choice format. Some have used a mixture of multiple-choice and short, constructed responses; others changed to multiple-choice, but later abandoned it in favor of the constructed short-answer format (Bude and Lewin 1997; Lewin and Dunne 2000).

Other reforms, particularly those related to the content of examinations, have involved much more radical changes. During the 1980s and 1990s, many countries, including Uganda (1983), Kenya (1985), Zimbabwe (1990), Tanzania (1994) (Bude 1997), and Namibia (1991 onward) engaged in examination reform. Following publication of the World Bank (1988) policy paper *Education in Sub-Saharan Africa,* which recommended "a renewed commitment to academic standards, principally through strengthening examination systems" (p. 93), the first plenary meeting of the Donors to African Education (DAE) (now the Association for Educational Development in Africa, ADEA) addressed the need to improve educational quality. This move reflected the mood and developments in many countries, and was followed by the establishment of a Working Group on School Examinations (WGSE) that recognized the important role that examinations could play in quality improvement. This in turn was followed in 1988 and 1989 by studies of examinations in 14 countries (Kellaghan and Greaney 1992). The objectives of these studies were to help improve the quality of education by developing more cost-effective systems of examination, and to help Sub-Saharan countries develop the institutional capacity to realize this.

Included among the examination reforms that have been recommended, as reported by Bude and Lewin (1997) and Kellaghan and Greaney (1992), are the following:

- broadening the scope of examinations to appropriately reflect the school curriculum;
- using diverse modes of assessment (written, practical, oral);
- redesigning examinations to include items that test higher-order thinking skills;
- assessing the ability of students to apply their knowledge and skills in situations outside school, as well as in a scholastic context;
- shifting testing from a norm-referenced to a more criterion-based approach (that is, measuring pupils' success or failure using criteria that assess competence rather than simply through reference to the performance of other examination candidates);
- incorporating teacher assessments into students' examination grades;
- incorporating into public examinations information from pupil records and profiles of achievement, to take account of learned competencies that cannot readily be assessed in a terminal written examination; and

- ensuring that the examinations differentiate between students on the basis of characteristics that are relevant to opportunities being offered.

These changes all seem desirable, and are capable of producing a more appropriate and valid assessment of student achievements.

Using Data from Examinations to Describe Student Achievements

Given the prevalence of public examinations in Africa, it seems reasonable to ask if the data obtained from these examinations could provide policy-makers and teachers with useful evidence about student achievements, including evidence of trends in standards of achievement. In addressing this issue, we describe three sources of information about examination performance: chief examiners' reports, other feedback mechanisms, and analysis to identify categories of pupils who perform poorly.

Chief Examiners' Reports

Analysis of student performance in examinations is a feature of many examination systems. The results typically are presented in a chief examiner's report, in which the strengths and weaknesses of the candidature, together with perceived deficiencies in teaching, are described. The extent to which these reports are used by key stakeholders is unclear. Reports vary considerably in quality, in the level of detail that they provide, and in the relevance of the information that they yield for individual schools and teachers.

The chief examiners' reports filed in Swaziland are not untypical of those provided in other countries (see Box 1). Based on primary and junior certificate examinations, the reports comment on broad areas of strength and weakness in student achievements, on teacher competence and curriculum implementation, and on how students' language competence affected their performance.

The role of language in instruction and, by extension, in examinations has received considerable attention in recent years, in both Anglophone and Francophone countries (Box 2). There can be no doubt that pupils are at a disadvantage when instruction is in a language, often a language of wider communication (LWC), in which they are not proficient (Naumann and Wolf 2001).

Specifically at issue is the extent to which language proficiency contributes to variance in candidates' scores that is not a function of their competence in the subject being assessed. The chief examiners' reports for Swazi examinations suggest that language proficiency was a factor in several subjects. Further evidence is available from a study in Burundi, in which stu-

---

Box 1. Chief Examiners' Reports in Swaziland

Reports on the Primary Certificate Examination noted poor levels of vocabulary and comprehension in English. Problems were also identified in the ability of examinees to construct sentences and in the use of grammar, spelling, and handwriting. In reading, there was evidence of poor ability to scan passages and locate relevant information. A facility in English is relevant not just to performance in the English examination, but also in other subjects. Performance in science, social studies, agriculture, and home economics was judged to have been affected by the inability of examinees to understand some words or questions.

Student proficiency in English was a persistent theme also of the reports on the Junior Certificate Examination. Again, this issue was significant not just in the context of performance on the English examination (poor sentence construction and use of tenses, poor punctuation and spelling, and problems answering questions involving inference, discussion, and symbolism all were noted) but also in the context of many other examinations. For example, failure to understand questions was noted as a problem for mathematics examinees; performance on the integrated science examination similarly was affected by the failure of students to understand questions and compose their responses.

In addition to analysis of candidate performance, the Swazi examiners reported their impressions of teaching and of curriculum implementation in schools They concluded, for example, that some schools had failed to fully cover the curriculum for integrated science, resulting in candidates avoiding physics and chemistry questions. Many areas of the metalwork curriculum (sheet-metal work, design, oblique projection) also apparently were not taught. In integrated science, there was evidence that in some schools, students had been given information that was factually incorrect. Review of the geography examination identified a need for students to have access to a greater range of books and other materials.

Source: Kellaghan 2002.

---

dent performances in reading, mathematics, science, and agriculture tests administered in French and Kirundi were compared. With the exception of mathematics, students obtained higher scores in the tests administered in Kirundi. It also was found that the performance of the most able students was most affected by being tested in French (Eisemon 1990; Eisemon and others 1993).

Box 2. Language of Instruction

Language is an issue not just in examinations. The use of a language of wider communication (LWC) for instruction also is significant, especially in subjects that have practical importance for the majority of primary school leavers who do not continue their studies. In many countries, most African community languages are not used in teaching, and in some countries, none at all are used (Ouane 2003).

In the Monitoring Learning Achievement (MLA) project, countries in which instruction was in the mother tongue of the students outperformed in most learning areas those countries in which instruction was not in the mother tongue (Chinapah and others 2000). A number of countries, including Mali, Niger, and Nigeria, as a consequence have introduced experimental programs in which instruction is in the children's mother tongue. Preliminary evaluation points to lower rates of repetition and dropout, improved performance on primary school leaving examinations, and higher transition rates for children (ADEA 1999; Bamgbose 1991). It is not possible to attribute these gains solely to language of instruction, however, as the student–teacher ratio in the experimental schools in the Niger study, at 22:1 to 25:1, was much smaller than the ratio (50:1 to 90:1) in traditional classes.

The rationale for the use of an LWC is complex, reflecting as it does concerns about national integration, cost, and international communication (Clayton 1998). An LWC may also have practical advantages in linguistically heterogeneous situations.

Other Feedback Mechanisms

A number of countries have developed systems of analysis and feedback to schools regarding pupil performance in examinations taken at the end of primary schooling. A reform of examinations in Kenya, for example, provided "guidance information" based on an analysis of the performance of candidates on individual items in the examination (Kyalo 1997; Rharade 1997; Somerset 1987, 1988, 1996). Advice was also provided on how to address problems that were apparent in candidate responses. The guidance information was provided in a newsletter sent to all schools and in workshops, seminars, and school visits, particularly to schools with poor results. The Kenya National Examinations Council continues to produce the newsletter, but the council's lack of financial resources means that it cannot be sent to all schools. The newsletter can, however, be purchased from the council (J. M. Mwachihi, personal communication, May 2003).

Feedback has also been a feature of other examination systems. In Zambia, every school was sent a copy of the chief examiner's report. In Lesotho, performance statistics for the population of examination candidates were sent to all schools (Kellaghan and Greaney 1992). And in Uganda, newsletters suggesting teaching strategies to address problems identified in examination performance were sent to schools.

Identification of Categories of Pupils Who Perform Poorly

Examination results can be used to identify differences in the performance of boys and girls, of regions, of locations (urban–rural), and of schools. It is not unusual to find schools in which practically all students are successful in their examinations and schools in which practically no students are successful. Although the reasons for these differences are complex and often involve sociocultural and student background factors that may not readily be manipulated by political action, the provision by educational authorities of guidance, support, and resources to poorly performing schools or districts nonetheless can lead to improvement. Analyses that reveal gender and regional differences can also provide a basis for a review of examination procedures to ensure that they are not biased against any subgroups of candidates.

Limitations of the Data Provided by Examinations

While analysis of examination results can provide insights into student achievement and can identify schools in which student performance is weak, its value is limited. One limitation is that public examinations usually test only narrow areas of a curriculum. This is partly because a limited number of subjects can be examined; it is also because within these subjects, the focus of the examination tends to be on curriculum content and competencies that will maximize discrimination between students who will be selected for further education and those who will not. The achievements of lower-performing students as a result may not be adequately represented.

The results of examinations also are sometimes used to monitor student achievements over time, to determine whether standards are rising, falling, or remaining constant. This use also is problematic. First, a different examination is set each year, and there usually is no way of knowing if the difficulty level of the examinations remains constant. Second, the results reported for examinations often are standardized and norm-referenced, reflecting their selective function, in which case the reported mean is fixed from year to year and so would not reveal a change in standards. Third, as the provision of education continues to expand (as is expected under EFA), and as more students sit for public examinations, the characteristics of examinees will change. This in turn potentially can affect the average level of achievement of the examinees, but the actual impact of increased participation is difficult to assess (Greaney and Kellaghan 1996a; Kellaghan 1996a).

Using Examinations to Improve Student Achievements

Analysis of examination results can provide some useful, if limited, information on student achievements. A more radical and proactive role for examinations is their use as a lever for reform. Proposals to use examinations in this way are reinforced by the fact that, when high stakes are attached to examination performance (that is, when performance has important consequences for students, and often for teachers), an alignment takes place between what is taught in schools and the objectives of the examinations. The case for what has come to be called "measurement-driven instruction" was made in the United States by Popham (1983, 1987), who argued that changes in assessment do not have to mirror changes in curriculum. If introduced first, the assessment changes can in fact be expected to drive curriculum implementation in schools. (It should be noted that this expectation runs counter to the traditional view that the content of an assessment should reflect the curriculum; a view, for example, that underlies changes made to the national examination and assessment system in Namibia that were considered necessary because of reforms to the curriculum [ADEA 1999]).

Several commentators on education in developing countries have seen a value in measurement-driven instruction as a means of changing classroom practice, given the high stakes attached to examination performance. The formula is relatively simple: Make sure that examinations cover important and relevant content and assess important knowledge and skills, and teachers will adjust their teaching accordingly. In this vein, Eisemon, Patel, and Abagi (1987) regarded the strategy of improving instruction through improved examinations as basically sound, while, according to Little (1982, p. 228), "examination improvements could help turn the education system into one which encourages, rather than stultifies, desirable outcomes." Heyneman and Ransom (1992) point out that changing examinations is not only a powerful means of influencing the quality of teaching and learning in schools, it also is an inexpensive one.

Effects of Changes in Examinations

The contention that by changing public examinations educators can improve the quality of student learning can be examined through closer investigation of the following questions:

- Will a change in the content areas examined result in a shift in the content to which students are exposed in class?

- Is a change in examinations likely to result in an improvement in the level of student achievements?
- Is a change in examinations likely to result in a change in the cognitive processing skills of students?

Will a change in the content areas examined result in a shift in the content to which students are exposed in class?
There is considerable evidence from numerous countries that changes in examinations affect the content of lessons; that is, the subjects that receive attention and the topics that are taught within those subjects. This has been the outcome when changes were made to chemistry examinations in Australia; to physics, mathematics, and chemistry examinations in Ireland; to the primary school examination in Belgium; to the New York Regents examination in modern languages; and to mathematics on the College Entrance Examination Board achievement tests in the United States (Madaus and Kellaghan 1992).

In Kenya, the introduction of Kiswahili and practical subjects to the Kenyan Certificate of Primary Education in the 1980s is reported to have resulted in a dramatic increase in the coverage of these subjects in schools, despite difficulties relating to facilities, textbooks, and teacher competence (Eisemon 1990). Also in the 1980s, Trinidad and Tobago amended its Common Entrance Examination, taken at the end of primary schooling, replacing a multiple-choice test on sentence style and structure by an essay-writing component. This had the effect of increasing the amount of writing tasks assigned by teachers, thus giving students experience in formulating arguments and applying their knowledge to problem solving. London (1997) reported that "essay writing has now been actively taught in the schools for almost a decade … [M]ost teachers … express a sense of relief that essay-writing … is being given its fair share of time within day-to-day classroom exercises" (144).

Is a change in examinations likely to result in an improvement in the level of student achievements?
There is little empirical evidence to support or to challenge the claim that a change in examinations will result in an improvement in the level of student achievements.

The most frequently cited study in this context is that of Somerset (1987, 1988), who examined the effects of changes made in the 1970s to the examination administered at the end of the basic education cycle in Kenya (see Box 3). The aims of the reform were (a) to improve the efficiency of the examination as a selection instrument; (b) to give less-privileged pupils (rural dwellers, children from low-income families, girls) a better chance of showing their abilities and hence of gaining access to secondary school;

(c) to encourage and help teachers to provide all pupils, and especially those who will not progress beyond basic education, with a more relevant set of cognitive skills; (d) to improve the overall quality of primary education; and (e) to reduce differences among districts and schools. To achieve these aims, the content of examinations was changed substantially, a school order of merit was published to put pressure on schools, and information on pupil performance in examinations was provided in a newsletter.

Box 3. Examination Reform in Kenya

In the 1970s, Kenya reformed its end of primary school examinations, to:

- reduce the number of items in tests that measured the memorization of factual information, and to add more items of higher-order skills, such as comprehension and the application of knowledge; and
- focus on the measurement of skills that can be applied in a wide range of contexts, in and out of school.

The changes were designed to affect the ways in which teachers prepared students for the examinations, and in particular to encourage the teaching and acquisition of competencies that would be useful to the majority of pupils who leave school after the examinations. Two types of information were provided to support these changes:

- Incentive information, comprising the publication of a district and school order of merit that was based on performance on the examination (league tables).
- Guidance information, based on an analysis of the performance nationally of students on specific questions. This information was published in a newsletter that was sent to all schools. The newsletter also explained changes in the content of and the skills assessed by the examinations, identified topics and skills that were seen to be causing problems, and suggested ways of teaching these problematic topics and skills.

League tables are no longer published, because schools and districts were found to be manipulating the system by presenting only their best students for examination. The Kenya National Examinations Council continues to produce a newsletter, but a lack of money means that it is no longer sent to all schools. It can, however, be purchased from the council.

Data are not available that would permit analysis of pupil performance since the reforms, as the scores each year were standardized (to a mean of 50 and a standard deviation of 15). Nor would a comparison of raw scores or pass rates be very meaningful, as there can be no assurance that the criteria for testing did not change over time. The performance data do, however, permit comparison over time of the relative performances of candidates in different districts. While the initial impact of the reforms was to widen the differences between districts, this trend was reversed after the system had been in operation for four years, when nearly all districts in which performance had been relatively poor showed striking gains relative to performance in other districts (Somerset 1987).

Is a change in examinations likely to result in a change in the cognitive processing skills of students?
A key objective of examination reforms has been to aid the development of higher-order cognitive processing skills. Many existing examinations assess mostly lower-level skills such as recall and recognition, with the result that it is these skills that are taught in schools. Should examinations require students to display higher-order skills, it is argued that teachers would change the content and methods of their teaching to develop these skills.

Evidence of the effect of examinations on the teaching and acquisition of higher-order skills is mixed. For example, Eisemon, Patel, and Abagi (1987) were unable, following changes in examination content in Kenya, to discern any move in primary school instruction toward addressing problem-solving, reasoning, or explanation. A study of two chemistry examinations in Swaziland (Rollnick and others 1998) found a similar lack of responsiveness on the part of teachers to the different kinds of questioning used. One examination (the Junior Certificate Examination, taken at the end of the junior cycle of secondary education) tested mostly recall and knowledge, while a later examination (O-level, at the end of the senior cycle of secondary schooling) assessed three cognitive levels (recall, knowledge with understanding, and the handling of information). The teaching in preparation for the examinations, however, was found to be basically the same. In both situations, teachers were concerned mainly with the acquisition of factual knowledge, and this was reflected in their use of low-level cognitive questions in class and in tests. Given that the O-level teachers used the same approach used by teachers at the junior secondary level, it is unsurprising that more than one-third of their students failed science (physics and chemistry) in the 2001 O-level examination (Kellaghan 2002).

According to Rollnick and others (1998), there is, however, some evidence that in-service provision could be effective in changing the approaches adopted by teachers. Guidance provided to teachers in the preparation of students for examination, coupled with the development of teacher understanding of the demands of examinations, can lead to greater emphasis on the classroom teaching of higher-level skills. In a study carried out in standard 8 in Nairobi primary schools, teachers were asked to prepare pupils for two sets of mock examination questions (Eisemon 1990). One set had been prepared by the Kenya National Examinations Council, while the other was designed specifically to test higher-order cognitive skills, requiring students to make inferences rather than to recognize the correct answer. The latter paper resulted in significant changes in the way in which teachers prepared their pupils, and these pupils ultimately performed better on both examinations than did those students who had been prepared specifically for the former examination.

Mechanisms to Bring about Change in School Practice and Student Achievement

Changing the format of an examination, changing the material that is examined, and changing the kinds of cognitive processing skills that are examined are steps that may in themselves impel changes in school practice. This is most true when the format of an examination is changed (for example, through the introduction of a practical element or the requirement that students write an essay as well as respond to short-answer questions). Any of these changes potentially can persuade teachers to respond to the syllabus and the demands of the examination by providing appropriate experiences for their students.

Some teachers, however, may require additional motivation to change, and others may simply be unable to change. Teachers, for example, may feel inadequately prepared to teach the practical elements of a science curriculum. Examination reformers and school authorities as a result have developed a number of procedures to induce change in teacher behavior. Some of these procedures rely on introducing or reinforcing competition between schools, some on providing information to schools, and some on providing additional guidance and/or resources.

Competition between Schools

Some examination systems seek to influence teacher behavior simply by publishing school examination results. The publication of "league tables" of mean performance statistics make it clear how schools stand alongside other schools in their district, and how one district compares with the next. This strategy, in which the published data were termed "incentive information," was a key feature of the Kenyan examination reform (Somerset 1987). The underlying theory was that the dissemination of information about school performance would create competition between schools that would motivate teachers to change their instructional practices (Chapman and Snyder 2000). It also was expected that the information would create a market situation in which parents would shop around for the best available school for their children.

There can be little doubt that assessment data published in league tables can affect the behavior of schools. In the 1990s, Senegal introduced a results-oriented management system, in which information on school performance was published in the press. Between 1995 and 1998, the success rate for the examination at the end of primary school rose from 30 percent to 48 percent. Furthermore, the enrolment rate of girls rose from 40 percent to 77 percent (ADEA 2002). These improvements cannot be attributed solely to the publication of results, however, as Senegal simultaneously introduced other reforms, including the introduction of job descriptions, more school inspections, and seminars and open days.

The use of results publication as a strategy to create positive competition may in fact be more complicated than it appears (see Box 4). Student achievements are dependent on a variety of influences other than those brought to bear by the school, and which may be outside its control. When students perform poorly, for example, it is reasonable to ask not just if the teaching is poor but also if the students are not motivated, have little home support, or the school is inadequately resourced. Furthermore, where students differ in their level of achievement when entering school, any subsequent measure of achievement that does not take this into account will be inequitable and misleading, in that it will not adequately reflect the school's success in moving students from their entry level to their level of achievement as reflected in a public examination (Kellaghan and Greaney 2001b).

Provision of Guidance to Schools

Student performance in examinations may be analyzed and the findings provided to schools. These findings may be furnished in traditional chief examiners' reports or, as has more recently occurred, in newsletters. A key feature of the newsletter that was produced following the Kenyan examination reforms, for example, was its provision of "guidance information" that identified topics and skills which were causing particular difficulties for students and that provided advice to teachers on how to deal with these problems (Somerset 1987, 1988). According to Somerset, the competitive aspect of the reforms was not enough; there was also a need to provide support and guidance so that teachers could reorient their efforts.

Support for Underperforming Schools

The provision of information about performance may be accompanied by the identification of underperforming schools, investigation of the reasons for

---

Box 4. Problems with League Tables

- The performance of schools (and thus their position relative to the performance of other schools) may vary depending on the school outcome that is used. School rankings will differ depending on whether they are based on public examination results, on performance in basic curriculum areas, on an assessment by school inspectors, or on an overall measure of school effectiveness.
- Rankings based on the same assessment can vary depending on the criterion of success that is used. A ranking based on the proportion of students who obtain high grades (honors or distinction) may differ from a ranking based on the proportion of students who achieve a moderate but acceptable level of performance, such as a basic passing grade.
- Lack of precision even in well-constructed assessment instruments can allow small differences between schools to affect outcome rankings. In a large school system, a difference of a few points on an outcome score between schools could result in a large difference in school ranking while in reality there was no difference between the schools.
- Whatever outcome measure is used, results can vary from year to year. In Britain, for example, the position of a school ranked within the top 250 schools has been known to change by as much as 123 places from one year to the next. This might be due to differences in measuring instruments, in the student cohort, or between teachers.
- Competition cannot operate when only one school is available in an area.

---

poor performance, and the provision of assistance to redress the problem. Work in these areas should seek to explain the meaning of school results (with reference, for example, to achievement objectives and the nature of student errors), and this in turn should lead to the provision of practical advice regarding the skills that need to be developed and types of exercises to be set. The relevance of the advice to the objectives being pursued should be visible in concrete terms, as reform efforts are more likely to be successful if teachers see the possibility of a direct return in the form of improved performance on the next examination (Grisay and Mählck 1991).

If it is concluded that poor performance is due to lack of textbooks, resolution of the problem may on the surface seem relatively straightforward. The provision of additional resources can introduce its own problems, however. Teachers who lack classroom materials adapt their teaching to this shortage, and it cannot be assumed that they will be able to change to make best use of additional resources.

Low achievement in any event stems typically from complex problems (Chapman and Snyder 2000) that may require complex interventions. Recognizing this, the reformers in Kenya instructed that district education offices should, based on performance results, advise schools on pedagogy and other issues (Somerset 1988). A further issue in dealing with poorly performing schools is that they are often in the most inaccessible locations, serving minority populations who have little influence on national politics (Chapman and Snyder 2000).

Linkage with Curriculum

At a broader level, the examining authority, ministry of education inspectors, and staff at curriculum centers should discuss examination results and their implications for curriculum development and implementation, teaching, and the preparation of textbooks. This was the practice in Kenya (Somerset 1988). Such discussion reflects an appreciation of the need for a close relationship between the examining authority and those responsible for the curriculum (Eisemon 1990).

Particular Problems When Assessment Information Carries High Stakes

Proponents of examination reform have argued that if the subject matter examined is extended and the taxonomic level of the cognitive processes required is raised, how and what students are taught in school should change accordingly. Somerset has said that "there is no intrinsic reason why the backwash effects of examinations on teaching and learning should be harmful; they are harmful only when the examinations are of inadequate quality" (Somerset 1996, p. 282). This view, while recognizing that the power of examinations to change school practice resides in the fact that high stakes are attached to performance, fails to take into account something else that has long been recognized: that whatever the quality of examinations, negative, if unintended, consequences can follow if sanctions are attached to performance (see Box 5) (Kellaghan and Greaney 1992; Madaus 1988; Madaus and Greaney 1985; Madaus and Kellaghan 1992).

The alignment of teaching with examinations is proposed as one of the advantages of high-stakes examinations, but a disadvantage of such examinations is that only a subset of an entire achievement domain is assessed. By focusing only on what is examined, schools deny to other subjects the attention that their place in the curriculum might suggest they merit. Furthermore, within a particular subject, teachers will tend to focus their

---

Box 5. How Teachers Are Influenced by Examinations

The extent to which examinations dominate teaching can be seen in the description of the not untypical behavior of teachers in Burundi. Eisemon (1990) described the following characteristics of teaching:

- an increase in instructional time beyond that laid down for primary schools (including, for example, Saturday afternoon classes);
- regular review of material that is considered essential;
- frequent testing to identify performance deficits and to improve test-taking skills;
- diagnosis of the sources of pupil errors, followed by a selection of appropriate instructional methods; and
- the use of class periods allocated to nonexamined prevocational skills, such as agriculture, for academic subjects that are examined.

Many of these features have been observed in the examination systems of other countries, particularly where examination results are an important determinant of future education and life chances or are used to evaluate teachers.

Source: Kellaghan and Greaney 1992.

---

instruction on the test content, leading to a narrowing of the curriculum and to a situation in which the examination becomes the manifest definition of the domain (Le Mahieu and Leinhardt 1985).

A further disadvantage of examinations to which high stakes are attached is that they tend to affect teaching strategies, learning strategies, student involvement in learning tasks, and student attitudes to learning. Teachers will tend to rely on drill, and may require their students to use strategies that are superficial or short-term, such as memorizing, rehearsing, and rote learning. Students will respond accordingly, and may focus on social comparison (that is, doing better than others), something that is demonstrated and reinforced by the common practice of applauding correct answers given in class. It furthermore has been found that when high stakes are attached to performance, students tend to be less successful in acquiring higher-order and transferable skills; learning tasks are perceived as not inherently interesting; and, if a reward is removed, students will be less likely to engage in a task (Kellaghan, Madaus, and Raczek 1996). Thus, attainment of some of the basic goals of education reform may be frustrated.

Another problem associated with high-stakes examinations is that they tend to create a focus on drill-dominated test preparation, including mock examinations. As a result, time is lost to instruction. In Guinea and Mali, it has been demonstrated that this lost time can amount to as much as a week per month in an examination year. Test preparation activities also can distort teaching and learning. For example, if an examination is made up of multiple-choice questions, teaching may reduce simply to the delivery of statements and a range of possible responses. The logical extension of this is that students concentrate on examination techniques rather than on developing a mastery of subject matter and on honing lasting competencies.

A further worrying aspect of high-stakes examinations is that these effects may not be limited to the educational experience of students at the examination grade. At lower grades also, the subjects in which the examinations are taken are likely to be given greater emphasis, at the expense of other curriculum goals. Even the format of examinations may affect teaching. For example, use of the multiple-choice format is observable not only in classroom tests but also in the teaching methodology applied in the early grades of primary school.

At a more general level, the use of high-stakes tests limits our ability to make inferences about improvements in student achievements. Student scores on an examination inevitably will rise where the teaching focuses exclusively on the material that is to be tested, but this improvement will be limited to those areas in which curriculum objectives overlap with test content (Le Mahieu and Leinhardt 1985). The result is goal displacement, as preparation becomes focused not on attaining curriculum objectives but on meeting the requirements of the examination. The effect of goal displacement is to distort the inferences that can be made from actual test performance: high performance, or an increase in scores, cannot be interpreted as evidence of high achievement in the broader domain of achievement that is envisaged in the curriculum (and which presumably an examination should measure). The examination therefore may be invalidated as a vehicle for assessing overall achievement (see Le Mahieu 1984; Linn 1983, 2000).

High-stakes examinations also may be associated with malpractice. In their efforts to obtain high scores, students (and sometimes teachers and others) may resort to cheating (Greaney and Kellaghan 1996b). Examination malpractice takes many forms, including copying from other students, collusion between students and supervisors, use of material smuggled into the examination hall, bribing or intimidation of examiners, and the purchase of examination papers (see Box 6). The pressure to cheat can be great, and while the extent of malpractice in examinations is not known, it is probably considerable: In one recent primary certificate examination in Uganda, the results of 3.16 percent of candidates were cancelled on grounds of malpractice.

Box 6. Some Forms of Examination Corruption

Prior to examination
Leakage of paper content by officials, paper setters, moderators, or school administrators; improper assignment of candidates to targeted centers.

During examination
Impersonation; external assistance (for example, from helpers or via cellular phone); smuggling of material (such as in clothing); copying and collusion among candidates; intimidation of supervisory staff (by candidates, external helpers, government agencies, politicians, journalists, and teacher unions); substitution of scripts; use of "ghost" (nonexistent) centers.

After examination
Substitution of scripts; intimidation of markers (sometimes with the aid of corrupt officials); reward seeking from parents; collusion between the candidate and the marker; falsification of data files and results sheets; issuance of fake diplomas.

Malpractice can erode the credibility of an examination system, and countries operate a variety of practices to combat it. These are primarily of three forms: prevention (such as having examination papers printed outside the country or keeping markers in isolation while scoring papers); detection (matching the response patterns of students who sit close to each other in an examination); and punishment—even in the form of prison sentences.

Finally, we should be aware of how high-stakes examinations can conflict with aspects of educational policy. For example, teachers, whose reputations may depend on how well their pupils perform in examinations, may focus their efforts on those pupils who are most likely to succeed. When this happens, it is likely to inhibit attainment of the Education For All goal that all pupils should complete a basic education of good quality.

A focus on achieving a high success rate on examinations may also lead to high rates of repetition and dropout, which are associated with high expenditure and low levels of internal efficiency (see Eisemon 1997; Madaus and Greaney 1985; N'tchougan-Sonou 2001). In Kenya, a low transition rate between standards 6 and 7 was partly explained by the fact that schools discouraged weaker pupils from taking the Kenyan Certificate in Primary Education examination, for fear that their participation would lower the school's mean score as published in the school league tables (Ackers, Migoli, and Nzomo 2001). Some pupils also may be held back in the belief that their repetition of one or more years will enhance their chances of passing their examinations and of going to secondary school. Repetition is a particular feature of Francophone countries, including Burkina Faso, Burundi, Cameroon, Chad, Comoros, Guinea, Guinea-Bissau, Niger, Rwanda, and Senegal. Government policies of automatic promotion (as operated in Kenya) are likely to be inhibited by high-stakes examinations.

Guidelines to Improve Public Examinations

Despite the drawbacks of high-stakes examinations, public examinations are unlikely to decline in prevalence or importance until education systems can accommodate many more students. The goal of reformers therefore should be to reduce the negative effects associated with these instruments. A number of guidelines, which if followed should serve to improve the quality of public examinations, are set out in Box 7.

Box 7. Guidelines to Improve Public Examinations

- Assessments should reflect the curriculum. Not everything in a curriculum can be assessed in an examination, so the areas that are assessed should be those that are considered most important. If the expectation is that student achievement will align itself with the content of examinations, it is critically important that the stated objectives and content be carefully developed. The objectives should reflect the contribution of knowledge and skill that they embody to the long-term growth and development of students (Le Mahieu 1984).
- As far as possible, the mode of assessment (for example, written, practical, or oral) should be diverse to reflect the goals of the curriculum.
- Examinations should not be limited to the measurement of recall or the recognition of information, but should attempt to measure higher-order outcomes defined in terms of more complex cognitive processes, including understanding, synthesis, and application.
- Examinations should assess the ability of students to apply their knowledge not just in a scholastic context, but also in situations outside school.
- Examinations, in terms of both content and difficulty, should reflect their certification function and should provide an adequate assessment of the competencies of pupils who will not obtain a higher-level qualification.
- Examination performance should be analyzed to provide feedback to schools and other stakeholders, including curriculum authorities.
- As many teachers as possible should be involved in the setting and scoring of examinations. These activities provide valuable insights into the demands of examinations, and these insights can in turn be applied in teaching.
- The possibility should be investigated of integrating teacher assessments as a component of the grading awarded in public examination.
- Examinations should be free of gender, ethnic, or location bias. The language used should not exhibit gender bias (for example, in the use of names), and topics that are included should be of interest to both girls and boys and should reflect situations that would be equally familiar to both genders. It should be noted also that there is evidence that the multiple-choice format tends to favor boys.

Source: Kellaghan and Greaney 1992.

3
National Assessments

Public examinations are a long-standing feature of education systems, but national assessments (sometimes called system assessments, assessments of learning outcomes, and, less appropriately, learning assessments) are relatively new (Greaney and Kellaghan 1996a; Kellaghan 2003; Kellaghan and Greaney 2001a, 2001b).

A national assessment may be defined as an exercise designed to describe the level of achievements, not of individual students, but of a whole education system or a clearly defined part of one (for example, grade 4 pupils or 11-year-olds). The centerpiece of the assessment is the collection of data in schools, primarily from students in groups responding to assessment instruments and questionnaires. Teachers may also be requested to complete questionnaires to collate information that is considered relevant to an interpretation of their students' achievements. The main elements of a national assessment are listed in Box 8.

National assessments were introduced in realization of the fact that the educational data on inputs to education that typically had been collected in the past were often of little relevance or use to educational planners (Kudjoh and Mingat 1993). National assessments would address this issue by providing information on the "products" or "outcomes" of schooling (such as student achievements or inequalities in the system). This information, it was hoped, could be used in conjunction with input data to provide a sounder basis for policy- and decision-making: National assessments would provide policymakers and decision-makers with relevant and reliable information about the state of the education system, its achievements, and its problems. The information furthermore would be amenable to analysis and interpretation. It would differ from that available from other sources, including that available from public examinations, which, while providing data on outcomes, do so only for those who take examinations. The information would also differ from that provided by research and education sector studies, which are generally short-term; national assessments hold out the possibility, if integrated into the overall management and administration of the education system, of provid-

---

Box 8. Main Elements of a National Assessment

- The Ministry of Education (MOE) appoints an implementing agency, either from within the ministry or an independent external body, such as a university department or a research organization, and provides funding.
- The policy needs to be addressed in the assessment are determined by the ministry, sometimes in consultation with key educational stakeholders (such as teachers' representatives, curriculum specialists, business people, and parents).
- The MOE, or a steering committee that it nominates, identifies the population to be assessed (for example, grade 4 students).
- The domain of achievement to be assessed is determined (for example, reading or mathematics).
- The implementing agency prepares achievement tests and supporting questionnaires and administration manuals.
- The tests and supporting documents are pilot-tested and reviewed to determine their curricular and technical adequacy.
- The implementing agency selects the targeted sample (or population of schools/students), arranges for the printing of materials, and establishes communication with selected schools.
- Test administrators (classroom teachers, school inspectors, or graduate university students) are trained by the implementing agency.
- On a specified date, the survey instruments (tests and questionnaires) are administered in schools.
- The survey instruments are collected, returned to the implementing agency, cleaned, and prepared for analysis.
- Analyses are carried out and a report prepared.

Source: Kellaghan and Greaney 2001b, p. 35.

---

ing on a continuing basis information that is relevant to education sector analysis.

The longest-running and best-known national assessments are in the United Kingdom, which has operated a system in one form or another since 1948; the United States, in which an assessment was first conducted in 1969; and France, which introduced a system in 1979. Also of long standing is the national assessment in Chile, which was first administered in 1978. These systems are all quite elaborate and collect information on a frequent basis. Assessment systems in most other countries are more recent and less elaborate (Kellaghan and Greaney 2001b).

Developments in national assessment in the world's less economically developed countries did not occur until the 1990s. Most of these developments seem attributable to the Declaration of the World Conference on

Education for All (EFA), which stressed that it is important to know what students actually learn through the educational opportunities provided to them (that is, what are the outcomes of education), and which emphasized the importance of better information as an input to more effective planning and management. The general unavailability of such knowledge indicated a need for national assessments and for the development of the capacity to carry them out.

Information Sought in National Assessments

All national assessments seek answers to one or more of the following questions:

- How well are students learning in the education system (with reference, for example, to general expectations, EFA goals, the aims of the curriculum, or preparation for life)?
- Is there evidence of particular strengths or weaknesses in the knowledge and skills that students acquire?
- Do the achievements of subgroups in the population differ? Are there, for example, disparities between the achievements of boys and girls, between students in urban and rural locations, students from different language or ethnic groups, students in different regions of the country, or students who drop out early or are repeating grades?
- To what extent is achievement associated with the characteristics of the learning environment (such as school resources, teacher preparation and competence, or type of school) and with the home and community circumstances of the individual student?
- Do the achievements of students change over time? (This can be particularly important at a time of major change in the system, such as when numbers are increasing or when new subjects or curricula are being implemented [Kellaghan 2003; Kellaghan and Greaney 2001b].)

Uses of National Assessment Information

The data provided by a national assessment have been used for a variety of purposes. These include:

- To bring to the notice of politicians, policymakers, and the public the need for more effective education (and perhaps additional resources) to promote social and economic development.
- To justify the allocation of discretionary resources. It should be realized, however, that there may be little flexibility in the way that resources can be allocated, as most resources go to teachers' salaries.

- To support policy decisions, such as those regarding grade repetition.
- To constrain "bad" policy decisions, such as the withdrawal of funding for in-service education, by placing issues in a broader context. Too many policy decisions focus only on a single dimension of policy.
- To identify, through examination of the findings of analyses of relationships between alternative inputs and student achievements, ways of making resource allocation more efficient.
- To improve management efficiency through increased accountability (and in some cases, through competition).
- To use the backwash effect of the assessment, as has been proposed in the use of public examinations, to ensure that teachers teach specific subject matter. This is only possible when all schools participate in an assessment and when sanctions are attached to performance (as is the case, for example, in Chile: see Himmel [1996] and Schiefelbein [1993]).

Variation in National Assessments

All national assessments have as a common objective the description of student achievements in the education system, but there is much variation in the ways in which they go about this (see Box 9). Different approaches to assessment have implications for the way in which the information derived can be used. For example, it would make no sense to attach high stakes to a school's performance (for example, by publishing results) if the assessment was based on a sample of schools; nor would it make sense to use the data from an assessment to judge the performance of individual students or teachers if each student took only a part of the test (as low as one-ninth in some assessments).

National Assessment Activity in Africa

In Africa, four major categories of national assessment can be identified. Three of these—the Monitoring Learning Achievement (MLA) project, the Southern Africa Consortium for Monitoring Educational Quality (SACMEQ) project, and the *Programme d'Analyse des Systèmes Educatifs des Pays de la CONFEMEN* (PASEC)—involve similar activities in several countries. The fourth category comprises national assessments, carried out in individual countries, that are not related to any of the three other projects.

The MLA Project

The MLA project, which began in 1992, is a joint UNESCO/UNICEF (United Nations Educational, Scientific and Cultural Organization/United Nations Children's Fund) initiative. It is part of the EFA assessment that has as its

---

Box 9. Differences in National Assessment Procedures

- Most assessments are based on a sample of schools and students, but in some countries, including Chile, France, and the United Kingdom, all or most students at a targeted age or grade are assessed.
- Each student may take only a fraction of a large number of assessment tasks, enabling the assessment to examine extensively the curriculum without requiring students to spend a lot of time responding to the demands of the assessment (as in Brazil, Ireland, and the United States); alternatively, all students may be required to respond to the same tasks (as in Uganda and Zambia).
- An assessment may or may not be designed to provide information about individual schools (or even individual teachers and students). When information is available about individual schools, an assessment may become a high-stakes operation, akin to a public examination (as is the case in the United Kingdom).
- Assessments differ in the complexity of the description of student performance. Results may be reported as a simple percentage of correct scores, or scores may be scaled using item response modeling.
- Assessments differ in the detail in which they describe performance (for example, subdomains may be used of the broader domain of mathematics or numeracy) and in the extent to which they attempt to establish relationships, some of which may be interpreted causally, between student achievement and factors such as school type or community characteristics.
- Assessments differ in the extent to which the data obtained from them are integrated into other aspects of the education system.

---

objective the construction of a comprehensive picture of the progress of countries toward the EFA goals (Chinapah 1997). In particular, it is a response to the need to monitor the extent to which students acquire useful knowledge, reasoning ability, skills, and values, as laid out in Article 4 of the *World Declaration on Education for All* (UNESCO 1990).

In MLA I, the achievements of grade 4 pupils were assessed in literacy (reading and writing), numeracy, and life skills (that is, awareness and knowledge of health, nutrition, sanitation, and hygiene). In MLA II, the achievements of grade 8 pupils were assessed in mathematics and science. Common tests were used in all countries. Both MLA I and MLA II collected data on students' backgrounds, including family backgrounds, and school characteristics.

To date, MLA assessments have been carried out in more than 70 countries, 47 of which are in Africa (UNESCO 2003a). Forty African countries participated in MLA I and 11 in MLA II. In Nigeria, results were presented by state. A regional approach was adopted in implementation to capitalize on local expertise and to develop capacity in participating countries. By March 2003, reports had been published on the MLA I assessments of 18 Sub-Saharan countries and on the MLA II assessments of 2.

In addition to the national reports, a separate single report has been prepared on the MLA I project in 11 countries (Botswana, Madagascar, Malawi, Mali, Mauritius, Morocco, Niger, Senegal, Tunisia, Uganda, and Zambia) (Chinapah et al. 2000). Only 4 of these countries had met their Jomtien learning target (that is, that 80 percent of learners should attain the defined learning competencies) for grade 4 pupils in life skills; only 2 countries met the target in literacy; and none in numeracy. Gender differences were small in all countries. With the exception of Mauritius, in all three learning areas, pupils in private schools performed better than did students in public schools. In most countries, the ability of parents to assist their children with their schoolwork was correlated with student achievement.

SACMEQ

The Southern Africa Consortium for Monitoring Educational Quality (SACMEQ) is a collaborative, voluntary grouping of 15 ministries of education in Southern and Eastern Africa. The consortium works in close collaboration with the International Institute for Educational Planning (IIEP) in Paris, with the goal of building institutional capacity through joint training and cooperative educational policy research (Ross et al. 2000; UNESCO 2003b). SACMEQ I was pursued between 1995 and 1998, when eight education ministries collected information on baseline indicators for educational inputs, general conditions of schooling, equity assessments for human and material resource allocations, and literacy levels among grade 6 students. Except in Mauritius and South Africa, both teachers and students were tested.

Between 1999 and 2002, 15 education systems participated in SACMEQ II: Botswana, Kenya, Lesotho, Malawi, Mauritius, Mozambique, Namibia, Seychelles, South Africa, Swaziland, Tanzania (mainland), Tanzania (Zanzibar), Uganda, Zambia, and Zimbabwe. Seven national reports have been published and 14 are in preparation.

A major aim of SACMEQ is to promote capacity building by equipping educational planners in member countries with the technical ability to monitor and evaluate schooling and the quality of education. Through providing valid and accessible information systems as a basis for decision-making, the consortium seeks also to promote stakeholder involvement and greater transparency. A particular feature of its approach is its learning-by-doing training for educational planners, whom it seeks to involve directly in the conduct of studies.

As in the case of the MLA project, the results of the SACMEQ assessments indicated that education systems were failing to meet performance standards of ministries. For example, in Namibia and Zambia, fewer than 30 percent of grade 6 pupils met the specified minimum literacy standards (UNESCO 2000a). Although in Zimbabwe more than 50 percent of pupils met "minimum" standards, this figure did not change over time (Machingaidze, Pfukani, and Shumba n.d.). Significant differences typically were found in the achievements of different regions and types of school within participating countries. Gender differences were not significant (Mioko 1998).

PASEC

The *Programme d'Analyse des Systèmes Educatifs des Pays de la CONFEMEN* (PASEC) was established in 1991 as a response to the Jomtien conference. PASEC acts as a network for the sharing among Francophone countries of information on educational evaluation instruments and results. It encourages the involvement of senior decision-makers and other stakeholders in the identification of policy issues, and emphasizes the need to base decisions on reliable data and to follow up these decisions with a realistic agenda for action, including time frames and cost estimates (Kulpoo and Coustère 1999). Initially only pupils in grades 2 and 5 were assessed, in French and mathematics. This has since been expanded to include pupils in all grades from 2 through 6. Data are also collected from pupils and teachers on a variety of school and background factors. Since 1994, the same tests have been used in all countries.

Twelve countries have participated in PASEC: Burkina Faso, Cameroon, the Republic of Congo, Côte d'Ivoire, Djibouti, Guinea, Madagascar, Mali, Niger, the Central African Republic, Senegal, and Togo. It has been estimated that PASEC and SACMEQ cost about US$50,000 per country (Kulpoo and Coustère 1999).

PASEC differs from other national assessments in Africa in that in some countries pupils are assessed both near the beginning (November) and at the end (May) of the academic year. It is thus possible to obtain some indication of growth or of the "value" added during the course of the year, though this is possible only for pupils who survive in the system. The approach reflects the strong research orientation of the program, which was in evidence at its inception, in its attempts to identify causal relationships on which to base policy that seeks to improve the efficiency and effectiveness of education. Efforts have been made to determine the impact of in-school factors such as teacher training, class size, and textbook availability as well as of nonschool factors, such as parental education, distance to school, and home language.

Other National Assessments

In addition to these three programs, several countries, including Burundi, Eritrea, Mali, Namibia, Senegal, Uganda, and Zambia, have carried out national assessments of their own. These vary in their technical adequacy. In Namibia, the National Learner Baseline Assessment measured student achievement in English and mathematics at grades 4 and 7 (Namibia Ministry of Education and Culture, Florida State University, and Harvard University 1994). Reading and listening comprehension were also assessed in Oshindonga, in a subset of northern schools. The assessment was designed to help policymakers allocate resources to underachieving schools; its results suggested that the expectation of competence in English was too high, and that curriculum materials might need to be revised.

As part of the EFA 2000 assessment, Eritrea tested pupils in six regions to determine if they had mastered, as laid down in the official curriculum, basic skills in their mother tongue (grade 1) and in English and mathematics (grade 4) (Eritrea Department of General Education 1999). The assessment identified aspects of the curriculum that were causing particular problems (such as place value, word problems in mathematics); found that boys generally outperformed girls; and identified implications for teacher education and teaching methodologies.

The Impact of National Assessments

Assessment teams (or close associates) have reported on the impact of all the assessment programs in a number of areas. In the areas of policy debate and formulation, SACMEQ results have featured in presidential and national commissions in Zimbabwe and Namibia, prime ministerial and cabinet reviews of educational policy in Zanzibar, national education sector studies in Zambia, and reviews of national education master plans in Mauritius (Ross et al. 2000). MLA results were used in the preparation of education reform programs in Malawi and Uganda, and PASEC results were used in country analysis reports in Burkina Faso and Niger.

The experience provided by the programs also is deemed to have contributed to capacity building. Following the MLA project, several countries, including Madagascar, Mali, Mauritius, and Morocco, carried out their own assessments. In Kenya and Zimbabwe, data cleaning methods used in SACMEQ were adapted for school census data; participant countries in the PASEC program similarly have been observed to have improved their capacity in test construction and in the design and execution of surveys.

The PASEC countries additionally have used information from the national assessments regarding grade repetition, class size, and textbook availability to support policy. To what extent this was justified is debatable: a reanalysis of data for Senegal, for example, attributed less importance to textbook availability than did the original analyses (Naumann and Wolf 2001).

Information from the national assessments has in some countries also contributed to national debate. For example, in Mauritius, SACMEQ data were used in a debate on strategies to mitigate the damaging role of the Certificate of Primary Education and to support an improvement in the pupil-to-book ratio. In the Seychelles, SACMEQ results initiated a debate on streaming.

In several countries the SACMEQ results have caused education managers to reappraise the adequacy of the resources provided for education. Kenya, for example, has introduced benchmarks—such as desks per pupil and books per pupil—for the provision of classroom facilities. In Zimbabwe, repairs have been made to school buildings, special funds provided for classroom supplies, and training programs initiated on the management of school libraries.

Assessment results, particularly where they have helped identify system weaknesses, have also been used to justify the granting of major donor support. In Guinea, for example, the results of the PASEC assessment prompted the national government and the World Bank to develop a program to promote instruction in local languages in the early grades. Gradual transition to French as the medium of instruction would take place in later grades.

The effects of national assessments should not, however, be overestimated. While experience with the MLA project has led some education systems to increase the weighting given in the curriculum to life skills, for example, there is as yet little reported evidence that this change has been translated into schoolroom practice. And in Mauritius, an external review team reported that relatively little had been done to act on policy suggestions made in three separate national assessments.

The present study posed a series of questions on the use of national assessment results to senior education personnel in six countries (Ethiopia, Malawi, Niger, Nigeria, South Africa, and Uganda). The respondents reported that while the findings of national assessments sometimes were covered in the media, in none of the six countries did they feature in parliamentary debate. In only one country were the findings used to justify the granting of additional resources to schools. In four countries, the results were shared with curriculum authorities, but in only two countries was feedback provided to teachers or schools, and in only one country was feedback provided to textbook publishers. Respondents in Ethiopia and Nigeria said that the national assessment results had not been used in the formulation of educational policy.

Issues in National Assessments

The decision to carry out a national assessment immediately raises a number of issues. Some of these need to be resolved before the assessment can begin;

others relate to the use and interpretation of data. This section draws on international experience to identify and describe 10 of the leading issues that are likely to arise.

Competence domain
A decision has to be made about the competence domain that will be the subject of the assessment. The two domains most commonly assessed are the language of instruction and mathematics (and less frequently science and social studies). One issue that merits consideration is whether the competencies assessed are based on the prescribed curriculum or on an appraisal of the knowledge and skills students will need when they leave school.

Population
Some national assessments involve pupils at one or two grades in primary school; others may involve pupils at all grades. Assessments at secondary school are less common but do exist.

All students or a sample of students
In some national assessment systems, such as that of Chile, all (or practically all) students in the relevant grades are assessed. Information therefore is available about all schools and teachers and about all students. This practice is used when action, such as the publication of results or the provision of support and resources to poorly performing schools, is planned at the school (or teacher) level. It is more common, however, that a sample of students will be selected for an assessment. This is considerably less expensive than testing all pupils, but the information obtained should be considered useful only for guiding policy formation and systemwide initiatives, and not to underpin intervention in individual schools.

Comparisons between regions or districts
Many countries are interested in comparing the performance of students in regions or districts. The assessment samples used typically are too small to allow meaningful comparisons, however.

Administer the whole test to all students, or subsets of the test to individual students
In several national and international assessments, students respond to only a fraction of the total number of items used. This diminishes the assessment burden on individual students, permits increased coverage of the curriculum, and enables the use of extended texts in reading comprehension. Other assessments require all students to respond to the same set of items. There are advantages associated with having students respond to only a fraction of the assessment but there are also disadvantages, partic-

ularly for countries beginning a national assessment program. Administration of a subset of the overall number of items is more complex, as is scoring and the scaling of scores; analysis of individual student or school data also is problematic.

Standards

The establishment of standards of competence, proficiency levels, or mastery levels ("minimal" or "desirable"), even when assessment instruments are described as criterion-referenced, is more problematic than much use of the terms would imply. There is no obvious basis for deciding on the point at which a standard can be said to be satisfied, and it is unreasonable to say that students who score just above a dividing point differ substantially in their achievements from those who score just below that point. Since the actual setting of standards usually is based on the judgment of individuals (which will always to some extent be arbitrary) (see Cizek 2001), and since the procedures involved can vary, the method used in standard setting always should be described. There is also a need to consider how criteria of competence in different assessment systems are related. Different standard-setting procedures usually produce different cut-points, even if each has a rational basis.

Data from public examinations and national assessments may reveal considerable discrepancies. For example, concern has been expressed in Senegal over inconsistencies between student scores on PASEC tests and teachers' promotional practices. Some students who did relatively well on the tests were not promoted, while others who did relatively poorly were (B. Moll, personal communication, May 2003). There are also differences between judgments made on the basis of performance on public examinations (Kellaghan and Farrell 1998) and judgments based on performance in national assessments. In Lesotho, where four out of five pupils passed the Primary Certificate Examination, fewer than one in six scored at the minimum level of mastery in a national assessment of literacy. In Malawi, close to four out of five pupils passed the Primary Certificate Examination, but in a national assessment, only one in five achieved minimum mastery. In Uganda, about 70 percent passed the certificate examination, but in a national assessment, only about one-third achieved minimum mastery. The figures for the examinations and national assessments are not based on the same cohorts of students, but the discrepancies are so large that it is unlikely that they do not represent real differences in the standards applied in public examinations and national assessments.

Monitoring over time

If student achievements are to be monitored over time, three conditions have to be met. First, the assessment instruments should be unchanged (or, if changed, the instruments used must be established as equivalent); second, unless the entire population is assessed, the probability samples must be determined to be of adequate size; and third, the definition of "standards" should be transparent. (It should be noted that the equivalence of instruments cannot always be maintained. For example, a curriculum may be changed to include content that is more relevant to students' lives, or to improve levels of understanding, analysis, and application).

Interpreting relationships
There is a tendency in some national assessments to make a causal interpretation of the relationships between inputs to the education system (such as school or student characteristics) and student achievements. Causal relationships on the basis of cross-sectional survey data are rarely justified. Furthermore, the facts that the numbers of schools/pupils in some categories (such as rural areas) are small and that the methods of analysis are inappropriate may mean that estimates are unreliable.

Capacity building
Experience suggests that it is difficult to retain trained, competent personnel for national assessment work. Such individuals often are promoted to more senior posts.

Stakeholder involvement
In some education systems, it may be difficult to secure support from the broader stakeholder community (teacher educators, teacher unions, minority groups) for a national assessment. Opposition from a stakeholder group can undermine an assessment.

Developing and Institutionalizing the Capacity to Conduct a National Assessment

A number of conditions and practices are required for the conduct and institutionalization of a national assessment (Chapman and Mählck 1993; Kellaghan and Greaney 2001b; Marope 1999; Samoff 1999). Central among these are the following:

- The need for information, including information about student achievements, and the need to develop the capacity to provide it should be recognized. Those who are in a position to make decisions about a national assessment and to provide the resources required to carry it out (for example, a minister or permanent secretary) must believe that the information will be relevant and useful in identifying problems and in informing policy and practice. Unless these decision-makers understand that a capacity gap exists and are prepared to address it, efforts to achieve the capacity to carry out and maintain a national assessment will fail.

- The knowledge and skills must be available to design, manage, and interpret a national assessment. Training, supported by adequate funding, may be required to develop this knowledge and the appropriate skills.
- An adequate level of support is required from all stakeholders, especially policymakers. Indications of a lack of institutional commitment to a national assessment include, for example, the transfer of trained personnel or the failure to commit adequate time or resources to the assessment.
- A national assessment should be integrated into the policy environment, specifically into existing structures, policy- and decision-making processes, and channels of resource allocation. It should not be seen as a separate activity that will cease when the assessment has been carried out. Full integration of the assessment into the policy environment is necessary to ensure that its findings reach those who have a role to play in formulating and implementing policy. The findings of too many sector analysis studies fail to reach key government personnel.
- Every effort should be made to ensure that the national assessment is aligned with other instructional guidance mechanisms in the education system. It should be aligned not only with other assessment systems, such as public examinations and classroom assessments, but also with the curriculum, teacher education, school capacity building, and measures to address inequities.
- Educational Management Information Systems (EMISs), where they exist and are operating, should be adapted to include data on the quality of student achievements as well as on inputs. This can help institutionalize assessment data and locate them in an environment in which they will come to the attention of policymakers and managers.
- Education authorities should establish systems and strategies of communicating with those individuals outside the ministry (especially teachers) who have a role in implementing policy that is based on national assessment data.
- Proposals regarding the use of national assessment data should be made in the context of a realistic understanding of the role of quantitative data in planning and management. Resource allocation and planning must always take cognizance of a variety of social, economic, and political factors.

4

International Assessments

International assessments have many of the same procedural features as national assessments. Where they differ most strongly is in the fact that they have to be designed to allow administration in more than one country (Beaton et al. 1999; Greaney and Kellaghan 1996a; Kellaghan and Greaney 2001b).

As is the case for national assessments, the instruments of international assessments are developed to assess student knowledge and skills. These instruments must, however, be appropriate for use in all participating systems. The age or grade at which the instruments are to be administered has to be agreed, as must the procedures for selecting schools/students. All international studies to date have been based on samples of students.

Since the 1960s, more than 60 countries have participated in international studies of achievement in reading, mathematics, science, writing, literature, foreign languages, civic education, and computer literacy. The studies give some indication of where students in a country stand relative to students in other countries. They also show the extent to which the treatment of common curriculum areas differs across countries, and this may lead a country to reassess its curriculum policy. Indeed, the main impact of international studies seems to have been on curriculum (see, for example, Burnstein [1993]; Kellaghan [1996b]; Romberg [1999]).

International Assessments in Africa

Few African countries have participated in major international studies. Ghana, Nigeria, and Zimbabwe participated in the IEA science study in 1983–1984 (Postlethwaite and Wiley 1992); no African country participated in the IEA reading literacy study; one (South Africa) participated in the 1995 Third International Mathematics and Science Study (TIMSS) and three (Morocco, South Africa, Tunisia) in the 1999 TIMSS-R; and one (Morocco) in the Progress in International Literacy Study (PIRLS). (It should be noted that these studies were designed for industrialized countries. Participation by African countries in international studies that are pitched to conditions and standards in the industrialized world would seem to be of little value.)

Students in South Africa performed poorly in both TIMSS and TIMSS-R: in TIMSS-R, the mean score recorded by South African students in mathematics at grade 8 was lower than the mean of the least proficient pupils in almost all participating countries. South Africa nonetheless was able to use the results to compare performance by province (Howie 2001) and to relate achievement scores to background variables such as home language, socioeconomic status, race, language of instruction, and student attitudes (Howie 2002).

The MLA, PASEC, and SACMEQ projects were designed as national assessments, but their results were reported in a way that would appear to permit international comparisons. To allow valid comparisons, however, instruments, target populations, sampling, and analyses would have to be identical in all countries. It is not clear that this was the case; for example, the MLA project involved the construction of "country-specific instruments" (Chinapah et al. 2000, p. 4). If the instruments varied from country to country, the interpretation of the mean scores for 11 countries that is presented in Chinapah et al. (p. 82) must be seen as problematic.

Problems Associated with International Assessments

A number of problems have been identified in international studies (Kellaghan and Greaney 2001b). These exist whether the studies are carried out in Africa or elsewhere, although some problems are more likely to arise in developing than in industrialized countries. The first problem that can be identified is that it is difficult to design an assessment procedure that will adequately measure the outcomes of a variety of curricula. Although there are common elements in curricula across the world, particularly at the primary school level, there are also considerable differences between industrialized and developing countries in what is taught and in expected standards of achievement. The greater the difference between the curricula and levels of achievement of countries participating in an international assessment, the more difficult it is to devise an assessment procedure that will suit all countries.

A second problem arises if it is necessary to translate the instruments of the assessment into one or more languages (this problem can also arise, of course, within a country). If comparisons are to be made between performances assessed in different languages, it should be realized that the differences that may emerge may be attributable to language-related differences in the difficulty of assessment tasks. It is very difficult to ensure that the way questions are phrased and the cultural appropriateness of content are equivalent in all language versions of an assessment task.

A third problem associated with international assessments relates to the equivalence across countries of the populations and samples of students that are being compared. This problem is most obvious where retention rates differ from one country to another, and so again is particularly relevant in studies in which industrialized and developing countries participate. There may also be more subtle differences related to population and sampling, such as the inclusion or exclusion, for example, of students in special education programs or with learning difficulties in one country, but not in another.

A fourth problem arises when the primary focus in reporting the results of an international assessment is on the ranking of countries in terms of the average scores of their students. This usually is the main interest of media. Rankings can be misleading when the statistical significance of mean differences in achievement is ignored. Besides, rankings in themselves tell us nothing about the many factors that may underlie differences between countries in performance (see Mislevy 1995).

Finally, while it might be argued that an examination of relationships between classroom inputs and student achievement is relevant, one cannot assume that practices associated with high achievement in one country will show a similar relationship in another. Relationships between inputs, processes, and outcomes need to be examined in the context of individual countries (Chapman and Mählck 1993).

There are thus many problems associated with international studies, but some countries nonetheless retain an interest in participating in such studies. There is much to be said for the experience that an international comparative study can provide in test construction, sampling, analysis, and report writing. Development and analytic costs, being shared, also may be lower. The South African experience with international assessment is also considered to have provided benefits in the form of increased private sector contributions to education, baseline information on standards in mathematics and science, and capacity building in educational research (see Box 10). However, it is not clear that the results of the assessment have significantly influenced policy in South Africa or have contributed to the development of sustainable national capacity in educational measurement—the latter point particularly so as members of the TIMSS and TIMSS-R teams since have moved to other positions (Howie 1999).

While individual countries may be interested in obtaining cross-country comparative data, there is much to be said for limiting participation in international assessments to countries that have similar levels of economic and social development. It should also be noted that many of the benefits of international cooperation can be obtained without going down the road of collecting international comparative data.

Box 10. South Africa's Experience with International Assessments

South Africa's experience with TIMSS and TIMSS-R underlines the problems facing implementers of international assessments. Howie (1999) noted that deadlines imposed by organizers can be difficult, if not impossible, to meet in situations where there may be no mail or telephone services or funds for travel to schools. Other problems include lack of accurate population data on schools; poor management skills; insufficient attention to detail, especially in editing, coding, and data capture; lack of funding to support project workers; and difficulty in securing quality printing on time. The instructions given to test administrators—for example, to walk up and down the aisle—also are obviously inappropriate where classrooms do not have an aisle.

5
Classroom Assessment

The assessment of student learning in the classroom, by teachers and by students, is an integral component of the teaching–learning process. Much of this assessment is subjective, informal, immediate, ongoing, and intuitive, as it interacts with learning as it occurs, monitoring student behavior, scholastic performance, and responsiveness to instruction. In addition to ongoing teacher observation, classroom assessment involves questioning and dialogue, the marking of homework, and the use of portfolios. Its function is primarily formative. It occurs during learning, rather than when learning is presumed to be complete, and is designed to assist or improve the acquisition of knowledge and skills. Its role is to determine the student's level of knowledge, skill, or understanding; to diagnose problems he or she may be encountering; to make decisions about the next instructional steps to take (to revise or to move on); and to evaluate the learning that has taken place in a lesson (see Box 11).

A key strength of assessment by teachers is its focus on performance. This emphasis has several advantages: it does not decontextualize knowl-

---

Box 11. Classroom Assessment

An official British publication reminds us of some of the basic roles of assessment in teaching and learning:

> [Assessment] can provide a framework in which educational objectives may be set, and pupils' progress charted and expressed. It can yield a basis for planning the next educational steps in response to children's needs. By facilitating dialogue between teachers, it can enhance professional skills and help the school as a whole to strengthen learning across the curriculum.

Source: U.K. Department of Education and Science and Welsh Office 1988.

edge and skills; it provides evidence of student learning in authentic settings; it allows an assessment of a student's ability to think critically, to cooperate, to solve problems, and to communicate; and it can contribute substantially to advancing student learning and understanding.

Classroom assessment may also be formal, as when teachers administer a quiz or end-of-term examination. Such assessment is more objective and can have a summative function, as, for example, when the information derived from the assessment is used to make a decision about the retention of a student in a grade or promotion to the next grade. The information may be reported to pupils, to parents, and to other teachers and individuals who may need to know about a student's progress. It also may be used to evaluate the appropriateness of the curriculum, of methodologies, of classroom organization, and of textbooks, as well as to provide guidance in matching the curriculum to the needs and abilities of students.

The Quality of Classroom Assessment

Despite the central role of classroom assessment in the teaching–learning process, we know little about how teachers assess their students. There is evidence, however, that the quality of classroom assessment practices may be deficient in many ways. Problems that have been identified include the use of poorly focused questions, a predominance of questions that require short answers involving factual knowledge, the evocation of responses that involve repetition rather than reflection, and a lack of procedures designed to develop higher-order cognitive skills (Black and Wiliam 1998; Madaus and Kellaghan 1992).

Observations of practice in African classrooms reveal a similar situation. One set of observations, made in a Kenyan study, relates to questioning, which is an important element in assessment. The study noted that in many lessons, pupils were asked no questions at all. When questions were asked, they were closed—a form of questioning that does not facilitate the development of higher-order thinking skills. Further, there was little assessment of pupils' understanding before the teacher moved on to the next part of the lesson (Ackers, Migoli, and Nzomo 2001). A study in Swaziland described the vast majority of questions in higher secondary classes as either rhetorical or at a low cognitive level (Rollnick et al. 1998). A low taxonomic level of questioning similarly was noted in primary classes in Tanzania; the questions asked were described as merely requiring of pupils to recall facts, which they did individually or in chorus (O-saki and Agu 2002).

In another area of classroom assessment, homework provides the opportunities for teachers to assess the proficiency of their students and to receive feedback on problems. The Tanzania study reported that little homework was given, however, for the reasons that in rural schools, textbooks or exercise books were not available, and in urban schools, large class sizes made it difficult to correct the work done. Furthermore, some teachers were observed to rarely mark their pupils' work—few exercise books contained teacher comments that might have provided reinforcement of good work or identified problems in poor work (O-saki and Agu 2002).

Several commentators attribute the assessment procedures that are prevalent in schools to the nature of the teaching–learning situation, which invariably is described as one in which the teacher is dominant and the pupils passive. Teachers have been described as talking nonstop throughout a lesson, leaving little room for pupil activities (Bude 1993). In the study involving classroom observation and interviews in primary schools in Tanzania, teachers were described as standing in front of the class and teaching pupils with expositions (O-saki and Agu 2002). A classroom interaction study of 102 lessons in Kenyan schools likewise found that teachers adopted a "transmission" approach that was similar for mathematics, English, and science, and in which there was little opportunity for pupils to become actively engaged (Ackers, Migoli, and Nzomo 2001). Lessons in science in upper secondary school in Swaziland also have been characterized as teacher-centered, with the teacher asking questions and pupils answering in chorus or individually (Rollnick et al. 1998).

Other explanations that have been offered for classroom assessment practices include the prevalence of poorly qualified teachers, large class sizes, poor facilities, and shortages of learning materials (including books) and of places to store them. Teachers in Guinea, for example, were reported to be poorly trained in assessment techniques, the classroom reality being "far from the continuous evaluation procedures recommended by official programs" (Carron and Châu 1996).

The negative influence of public examinations on teaching and assessment has also been noted. Eisemon, Patel, and Abagi (1987) observed that pupils were taught through drill, recitation, and exercises of a fill-in-the-missing-word type, all of which procedures were designed to impart the factual information and techniques that the students would need in a public examination. The use of mock examination papers also was criticized for limiting the scope of instruction to what the teacher thought would be examined, and therefore for leading to lessons that were incoherent. It is also likely that, while the causes and effects of repetition and dropout are complex, classroom assessment practices and public examinations contribute to them (see N'tchougan-Sonou 2001).

Improving Classroom Assessment

If these observations on classroom assessment represent general practice, or even a significant amount of practice, in schools in Africa, assessment practices and the approach of teachers to instruction must change. This is essential if assessment is to contribute significantly to the improvement of student learning. Teachers must increase their efforts to encourage the active participation of students in learning, they must involve students more in the teaching–learning process, and they must insist that students share responsibility for their own learning. At a more fundamental level, teachers may need to appreciate that learning is more than improved examinations results, more than the acquisition of information, and that learners should not only acquire, but also generate, master, develop, and create knowledge (Samoff 1999). Anything that can move education systems— preservice, in-service, or reformed public examinations—toward these goals is to be welcomed.

With some notable exceptions in Francophone countries, classroom assessment has received little attention in reforms that propose the use of assessment to improve student learning. This may be because classroom assessment is difficult and expensive to reform, but given its central role in the teaching–learning process and the disadvantages associated with high-stakes public examinations, its reform should be accorded high priority in any program that aims to improve student learning (see Box 12). Furthermore, any efforts made to improve classroom assessment should be coordinated with reform efforts in other assessment systems.

Given the complexity of classroom assessment, and based on the evidence relating to teacher skills and practice in this area, there is an obvious need for infrastructure that can support the improvement of assessment quality. This infrastructure should engage all stakeholders who have influence over classroom teaching and assessment practices (such as school inspectors, curriculum developers, those who set examinations, and textbook authors) and should embrace preservice and in-service training for teachers and possibly the provision of assessment materials to schools. The latter might include tests and item banks; for example, in South Africa, Assessment Resource Banks (ARBs), which comprise a set of tasks designed to assess specific learning outcomes, are provided to schools in areas serving pupils from low socioeconomic communities. The ARBs require that adequate records of pupils' progress be kept in individual learner profiles and that regular reports be provided to school principals. The principals in turn must provide regular reports to district education offices (Kanjee 2003). In Swaziland, materials provided to schools include general information about classroom assessment, item banks, tests, item specifications, and remediation and enrichment materials (Mazibuko and Magagula 2003).

Teacher education programs should include a component addressing student assessment. Trainee teachers should be introduced to the concepts underlying assessment and should learn about the use, interpretation, and

---

Box 12. Suggestions to Improve Classroom Assessment

The following are a number of suggestions designed to improve classroom assessment procedures. They may also be used to inform teacher education courses.

- Assessment should be an integral and frequent aspect of teaching, and should feature questions that focus on meaningful aspects of learning.
- Teachers should set reasonable but attainable expectations for all pupils.
- The focus should be on diagnostic and formative aspects of assessment, rather than on normative aspects such as the ranking of students on the basis of results.
- Teachers should ask questions that require students to exercise higher-order thinking skills (not just recall) and that call for inferential and deductive reasoning.
- Pupils' understanding of the general principles of a curriculum domain should be assessed, as should their ability to use appropriate methods and strategies in problem solving.
- Clear and prompt feedback should be provided to students.
- The way that students approach and analyze problems, rather than just the product of their work, should be assessed.
- Assessment should encourage students to reflect on their own learning.
- Questions should require students to explore the issues raised, not merely to repeat information.
- The results of assessments, where appropriate, should be communicated to parents and other interested parties (for example, other teachers).
- The use of criterion-referenced tests can enrich classroom assessment practice. Periodic administration (every few weeks) of such tests can provide information on what students have learned, can help identify situations in which there is a need for further teaching, and can help identify students in need of additional help.

---

appropriateness of a range of formal and informal techniques designed to assess the progress made by students and to diagnose difficulties they may be encountering. They also should learn how to address any such difficulties: courses should be provided that draw on college resources in psychology, education, and teaching practice.

The Use of School-Based Assessment in Public Examinations

The discussion thus far has considered classroom assessment in the context of day-to-day teaching, in which information derived from assessments is used primarily for formative purposes. Assessment data generated in the classroom also can be used for summative purposes (usually referred to as school-based assessment or continuous assessment), in which the data contribute to the grade ultimately awarded to the student in an external public examination.

By contrast with teachers' assessment in the classroom, public examinations are limited in the time frame in which they are administered, in the knowledge and skills that are assessed, and in the techniques that are used. Any of these limitations could result in students not being given the opportunity to demonstrate their true level of competence.

To address this situation, several examination systems in Africa have introduced or are planning to introduce an element of school-based assessment to their public examinations (see Box 13). At the primary-school level in particular, some of these systems are seeking to replace external examinations entirely with school-based assessment, perceiving it to be the only way in which the range of competencies specified in the curriculum can be validly assessed, and in which the negative effects of external examinations on teaching and learning can be removed. This approach, however, is problematic for a number of reasons, including that, in a system in which secondary school places may be limited, school-based assessment may be perceived as being a less than objective means of selection.

Arguments have been advanced both in favor of and against the use of the results of school-based assessment to determine student grades in what is primarily an external examination (Bude 1997; Heyneman 1988; Kellaghan and Greaney 1992; Pennycuick 1990a, 1990b; Wasanga 1997). The main arguments supporting the use of school-based assessment are as follows:

- Since school-based assessment is carried out over time and by a person who knows students well, it is likely to provide a more valid and reliable appraisal of a student's achievements than is possible in a single external terminal examination.
- School-based assessment permits examination of a larger range of curriculum topics. Aspects of achievement that cannot be satisfactorily assessed in a terminal examination include a student's ability to plan and organize a project and persevere with it over time. While the assessment of oral and practical skills may be carried out in an external examination, such examination inevitably will be limited, artificial, and expensive.

Box 13. Continuous Assessment in Swaziland

Continuous assessment has for many years been proposed as a way of improving the quality of education in Swaziland. In the 1980s, a conference of senior school and ministry personnel proposed that (a) continuous assessment should deal with noncognitive as well as cognitive development; (b) national item banks should be available to teachers to construct tests; (c) clear guidelines for assessment should be provided; (d) procedures for recording and interpreting should be common to all schools; and (e) standards should be controlled statistically and moderated in school inspections.

Continuous assessment was piloted in 16 schools in 1991 and 1992, and in 1993 was introduced to all primary schools for English and mathematics. Problems encountered included large classes and an associated lack of time to administer assessments; lack of teacher competence, especially in the case of unqualified teachers; lack of remedial teachers to provide a backup service; and the limited value for parents of reports based on the assessments.

Nevertheless, review of the public examination system by the Examinations Council of Swaziland and the National Curriculum Centre in 1994 set in motion the process of incorporating aspects of continuous assessment by teachers into the public examinations system. A mark based on continuous assessment has for several years now contributed 5 percent to a student's score on the Primary Certificate Examination.

- School-based assessment reduces the undesirable backwash effects of external examinations, since grades are not determined solely on the student's performance on the examination.
- School-based assessment can make allowance for a performance on an external examination that may be untypical of the student, due, for example, to illness.
- School-based assessment, if spread over the year, can increase the level of pupil motivation and application throughout the year.

The main arguments against the use of school-based assessment in examinations when results are used for certification or selection are as follows:

- The use of school-based assessment can change the nature of the relationship between teachers and students from an essentially supportive and collaborative one to a judicial one.
- The competence in assessment of many teachers is considered to be poor. Even where it is not, teachers often are uncertain how to translate their

informal judgments into formal, public assessments. The danger is that they may fall back for their assessment on poorly constructed tests or may draw on the multiple-choice tests contained in some textbooks.

- The standards used to grade students in school-based assessment are likely to vary, both between schools and between classes within schools. Teachers tend to assess their pupils with reference to other pupils in their class, rather than with reference to pupils in other schools, but it is essential that public examination results be based on comparisons that are valid across schools. To address this issue, school-based assessment results may be moderated or scaled against written examination results, as is the case in Namibia. This, in effect, privileges the external assessment by making the school-based results conform to the standards and distributions displayed in the written examination.
- School-based assessment can subject teachers to considerable parental pressure, particularly in small and closely knit communities.
- School-based assessment requires teachers to devote considerable time to assessment and record-keeping. It may be considered by teachers to involve too much work.
- School-based assessment gives rise to a variety of administrative problems for schools, such as what to do when students are absent for tests or when students transfer from one school to another.
- Teachers' assessments are subject to a variety of biases relating to gender, socioeconomic background, and even personality.
- It is difficult, in some cases impossible, to apply school-based assessment to non-school-based candidates.

It is hardly surprising in light of these observations that the implementation of school-based assessment as a component of public examinations, in countries including Lesotho, Namibia, Nigeria, Swaziland, Tanzania, and Uganda, has proved problematic. While the aspiration and motivation to introduce it have been high, the practical difficulties have on more than one occasion resulted in the failure, postponement, or limitation to a token amount of the school-based element. In Namibia, the school-based element contributes between one-third and one-half of the score in student grading (V dMerwe 1999); in Swaziland, it contributes just 5 percent to student grades on a public examination (although it is hoped to increase this proportion to 50 percent) (Kellaghan 2002).

The privileged status accorded to external assessment is not limited to the way school-based assessments are moderated against performance in the external component of an examination. Because of problems associated with teacher competence in assessment and with the interpretation of teacher assessments, there has been a tendency in countries that have incorporated school-based assessments into their public examinations to focus on the formal aspects of assessment in schools, rather than on the informal aspects. As a result, the schoolroom assessment may end up based on written tests or item banks administered to pupils in a formal test situation that essentially mimics the external examination.

The only advantage associated with this practice would seem to be that it gives pupils more than one opportunity on which to display their competence in a written examination. It unfortunately ignores the primary purpose of incorporating judgments based on school-based assessment into public examination grades: to provide teachers, who know their students well, with the opportunity to assess their competence in a variety of situations, using a variety of modes, over an extended period of time, in areas of the curriculum that cannot be assessed in a written examination.

6
Using Assessment and Examination Information in the Classroom

There is much to commend in the use of data from examinations and national assessments to provide feedback on student performance. However, there is a clear need to move from the macro to the micro level in the use of this information. While there is broad agreement that, in the words of Verspoor (1992, p. 23) "educational reforms live or die by the success of their implementation at the school level," educational planners invariably do not pay adequate attention to implementation issues.

Getting information to teachers and effecting changes in teacher behavior is difficult, and expectations that information from assessments and examinations will radically alter the culture of schools and substantially raise the achievements of all students often are unrealistic. There are numerous factors that can frustrate the intentions of reformers, which, if not recognized and addressed, can severely impair the potential of assessment-based policies to improve student learning. The factors discussed in this section are relevant whether educational reforms are based on public examinations or on national assessments.

Mode of Intervention

The most common mode of intervention involves centralized decisions regarding the input required to bring about desired behaviors in schools. Centralized decision-making can be appropriate when problems are well structured and the solutions to them—such as the provision of textbooks—are universally applicable. It is less likely to be appropriate when problems are not clearly defined and when their solution requires a multiplicity of responses that will vary according to local circumstances. This is the case, for example, when problems relate to instructional objectives, equity, and quality. In such circumstances, an indirect and interactive strategy, typically relying on enabling and framework-setting legislative and administrative measures, together with locally targeted financial and professional support, will be required (Verspoor 1989, 1992).

Relevance of Information

There are a number of inherent limitations on the use of data derived from examinations and national assessments to guide the practice of individual teachers. First, since the data relate to general standards of student performance, they may not be relevant to a consideration of conditions and student achievement in an individual school. Second, items in examinations and assessments and the data derived from them are limited in the extent to which they can provide insights into the knowledge structures or cognitive strategies on which they call. And third, since these items are not designed to be diagnostic at the level of the individual, analysis based on results will provide little instructionally relevant information about individual students. The extent to which they can provide specific guidance to teachers therefore is limited.

Teacher Competence

Assumptions that all teachers teach in a coherent and organized way (that they focus on the instructional targets of an examination, for example) and are capable of change, and that classroom conditions allow teachers to teach in a way that will meet the objectives of reform, may be based on an unrealistic perception of classrooms.

Carron and Châu (1996, p. 202) describe the "chaotic reality" of classrooms: "[T]eachers and pupils are often absent, the teacher does not have the competence required to teach well, he/she does not follow a precise work plan, merely reads from the textbooks, does not use the blackboard ... ." Other commentators similarly note a lack of teacher competence. Many teachers have a poor command of the language of instruction and weak knowledge of subject matter (this is particularly true in science and agriculture). Almost one-half of South African mathematics teachers do not possess a formal qualification in their subject (Arnott and Kubeka 1997), and the Monitoring Learning Achievement (MLA) regional study found that fewer than one in four teachers in Madagascar, Malawi, and Mauritius had any post-secondary education (Chinapah et al. 2000). A chief examiner's report on the Junior Certificate Integrated Science Examination in Swaziland said that there was evidence in examinees' scripts that in some schools, students had actually been given information that was factually incorrect. These observations may relate to extreme and exceptional cases, but the problems described are precisely the ones that will need attention in any reform effort.

Teachers' Understanding of the Implications of Change

The gulf between what reforms require of teachers and what teachers understand of those reforms and can achieve can be large. It cannot be assumed that teachers will know how to respond to assessment results. Even when provided with guidance, teachers may develop a different understanding of the objectives of reform than that which is held by policymakers, as they are likely to interpret the guidance in the context of their existing understanding of curriculum and instruction, which may be very different from that of the reformers (Chapman and Snyder 2000; Grant, Peterson, and Shojgreen-Downer 1996).

In Uganda, for example, teachers failed to understand the implications for classroom practices of changes made to examinations. Uncertain of how to proceed, they refused to take chances with the new instructional strategies and so did not change (Snyder et al. 1997). Similar findings are reported from Trinidad and Tobago in a study involving classroom observation and interviews with teachers following changes in public examinations (Chapman and Snyder 2000). It was found that teachers who depended on memorization and group recitation did not know how to modify their teaching to develop student competence in problem solving. They struggled to understand the implications of the test changes for their day-to-day classroom practice, and as a result, so too did their students fail to grasp the implications of the changes (see Box 14).

Providing teachers with the information and skills necessary to adapt to change can be difficult. It is clear that teachers may need considerable continuing support in their effort to understand reforms and to devise appropriate strategies to meet the goals of those reforms.

Box 14. Teachers' Difficulties in Adjusting to Changes in Examinations

The main finding of a study in Trinidad and Tobago was reported by Chapman and Snyder (2000, p. 362), as follows:

> … teachers could not necessarily adjust to the examination changes. Even if they understood the examination requirements at a cognitive level, they were often unable to make the necessary changes in the classroom to improve their students' performance. Moreover, experimenting with new pedagogical approaches was threatening to teachers, who felt under enormous pressure to look good and show good local test results. … For many teachers, the route to improved examination scores seemed too uncertain and taking chances with new teaching techniques seemed far too risky.

Complexity of Teaching

Teaching can be an extremely complex activity, requiring teachers to interact with a large number of learners who vary in their levels of achievement, aptitude, motivation, and interest. The rules that govern this interaction are not simple, linear, or obvious (see Box 15).

Furthermore, teachers may have to employ a multiplicity of strategies when addressing problems associated with poor achievement. Even when students register the same level of achievement on a test, the nature of their achievement, the reasons for it, and the learning difficulties that it implies can be very different, and can require different kinds of treatment (see, for example, [Buly and Valencia 2002]).

Particular problems arise when examinations, as they increasingly are designed to do, emphasize the measurement of higher-order skills. The teaching of such skills differs in many ways from the teaching of lower-level ones: they cannot be taught by rote methods; they take longer to teach; they develop gradually over time; they are less amenable to direct instructional approaches; they are often difficult to locate in a curriculum; and they may be too diffuse to drive instruction (Airasian 1988). This does not mean that they cannot be taught. A study in Nigeria found that when primary school pupils were taught social studies using a problem-approach method, not only did they acquire more facts but they also better understood the material and were better able to apply their knowledge to the solution of new problems and to evaluation activities (Ogundare 1988).

Classroom Context

Reforms that involve change in teaching style must take into account class size and the availability of teaching aids. Where classes are large and

---

Box 15. The Complexity of Teaching

"The key components of classroom instruction are not distinct, static behaviors, but rather are dynamic patterns of behavior that follow the ebb and flow of classroom activities and atmosphere. The connection between changing tests to changing instruction is not a technical relationship in which a shift in test format, content, or item complexity necessarily signals any particular change in that dynamic process. Moreover, changes in individual teacher behaviors do not necessarily translate into changes in student learning."

Source: Chapman and Snyder 2000, pp. 462–463.

resources few, as is common in Africa, this is of particular importance. The shortage of textbooks means that students may seldom study from printed texts; teachers instead may summarize the texts, transforming passages into class drills and assignments to be copied into their pupils' exercise books (Eisemon, Patel, and Abagi 1987). In Kenya, technical subjects such as crafts and domestic science were added to general subjects in the primary school curriculum in 1983, with the objective of facilitating the teaching of techniques, knowledge, and skills that would be useful for economic growth by enabling pupils to proceed to vocational training or start their own business. By 1990, only 3,000 of the 13,000 required laboratories had been built (Rharade 1997).

Opposition Based on the Perception that a Change Will Involve a Risk to Pupils

Parents and teachers may perceive changes in classroom practice, and in assessment procedures in particular, as a threat to the advantage that the existing system gives to their children (Chapman and Snyder 2000). While supportive of steps that they perceive to improve the quality of education, they may in practice be more concerned about maintaining the comparative advantage that their children enjoy under existing conditions, fearing that they will do less well in an alternative system or will suffer while teachers strive to adapt.

7

Conclusion

Improvement of the quality of education has, over the past decade, been a key feature in developing countries of reform proposals made by governments and donor agencies. While the term "quality" may be applied to many aspects of education, outcomes or student achievements—the acquisition of "useful knowledge, reasoning ability, skills, and values"—were assigned a central position following the Declaration on Education for All at Jomtien in 1990.

This paper described four areas of assessment—public examinations, national assessments, international assessments, and classroom assessment—all of which have to varying degrees figured in reform proposals. Two of these, public examinations and classroom assessment, are long-standing and important features of education systems in Africa. Both have as their primary focus assessment of the achievements of individual students. National and international assessments, in contrast, appeared on the educational scene in Africa only in the last decade, and have as their primary focus the assessment of the achievements of the education system.

Public examinations have received the most attention in proposals that would use assessment as a lever of reform to improve student achievements. On the basis that, when important consequences are attached to the performance of students and teachers, the content and form of examinations immediately and directly affect what is taught and learned in schools, a variety of reforms and innovations have been proposed. The reforms have four major thrusts, to:

- improve administrative efficiency, for example, through the introduction of computerization and optical scanning;
- improve the quality of examinations by removing obvious deficiencies, such as limited curriculum coverage and a focus on recall and recognition;
- include topics in examinations that would be useful to the many pupils who do not go on to secondary school, and so remove the bias toward the selection function of examinations; and

- change the content and taxonomic level of questions in examinations to include items that measure higher-order thinking skills and the ability to apply knowledge and skills in new situations (a reform that should benefit both students who leave school after the examination and those who will continue with their formal education).

On the basis that teachers "teach to the test," it has been argued that implementation of these reforms would be reflected in what and how teachers teach, and that this in turn would be reflected in the achievements of students. To strengthen the impact of the reforms, a number of education systems have provided feedback to schools based on an analysis of candidature performance on examinations, identifying areas of work that are in need of attention. There can be little argument against these proposals, which all examination systems would do well to implement.

Many of the needed reforms in public examinations could be achieved at little or no additional cost. Implementation could be assisted in a number of ways, including through twinning relationships with overseas agencies to obtain technical assistance, and through the development of closer working relationships between examination boards, which already exist in some regions in Africa, to facilitate staff exchange and monitoring of standards. Regional capacity development initiatives could also explore ways of maintaining standards, combating malpractice, and teaching new assessment and scoring techniques.

While reforms and innovations may be expected to improve the quality of examinations, it should not be assumed that, because poor assessment can narrow the curriculum and depress standards, better assessment automatically will enhance the curriculum and raise standards (Torrance 1997). The available evidence suggests that if the content areas of examinations are changed (for example, if a new subject or a new component of a subject, such as essay writing, is examined), the content to which students are exposed in class will also change. The evidence regarding changes in student achievement levels and cognitive processing skills is less clear. Where improvements do occur, they are likely to be modest.

These findings should not surprise us. Many students currently perform poorly on examinations, but this clearly is not due solely to the quality of the examinations. Much more significant is the prevailing lack of teacher competence and lack of resource material, the large size of classes, and the difficulty of teaching higher-order skills. It is unrealistic to expect that new examinations can override the influence of these factors.

The fact that some examination reforms are being driven by mechanisms involving high stakes, such as selection, competition, and the publication of results, raises questions about the negative (if unintended) consequences that might be expected. In particular, there is a danger that the greatest benefits will accrue to high-achieving students. This will happen if teachers, seeking to improve their success rate, focus their efforts on those pupils who are most likely to succeed; if low-achieving pupils are retained in grade to prevent them sitting the examination; and if discouraged students leave school before completing primary education. These are all serious issues in the context of the Education for All (EFA) policy, which has as its objective ensuring that "recognized and measurable learning outcomes are achieved by all, especially in literacy, numeracy, and essential life skills."

The conflict between the traditional function of examinations, which was to select the highest-achieving students for further education, and the goals of EFA, which express concern for all students, needs to be recognized, and steps need to be taken to ensure that examinations do not block realization of these goals. It is important to ensure that examination reform does not impede quality improvement but supports it, by, for example, extending curriculum coverage, including material relevant to the everyday life of students and the needs of the economy, and ensuring that examinations reflect their certification function by including content that is appropriate for all levels of student achievement.

The limitations of public examinations, which arise from the narrow range of knowledge and skills that they assess and from the fact that high stakes are attached to student performance, are to some extent addressed by incorporating teachers' assessments into the grades awarded in public examinations. While several examination systems have taken or are taking steps to do this, there are many problems associated with the practice. These problems render it unlikely, given the shortage of places available at higher levels of educations, that school-based assessment can entirely replace the role of external examinations in pupil selection.

The primary purpose of a national assessment is to describe student achievements in the education system, but it is envisaged that assessment also can play a role in improving educational quality. The information obtained in an assessment about strengths and weaknesses in the knowledge and skills that students acquire, and about how achievement is distributed in the population (for example, by gender or location), can play an important role in informing policymaking and decision-making (relating, for example, to resource allocation). A national assessment can also provide information that is relevant to curriculum developers, textbook writers, politicians, and indeed the general public, making assessment a lever of reform as well as a means of simply describing conditions.

Much of the activity relating to national assessment that took place in Africa during the 1990s would seem to be due primarily to the impetus of the 1990 World Conference in Jomtien and to the resources provided by international agencies and other donors. If this is indeed the case, there are questions about the extent to which policymakers and planners in individual countries perceive a need for assessments, and about their sustainability. The fact that several countries have had as many as three separate national assessments, each sponsored or supported by a different agency, would suggest that the assessments were not undertaken in response to locally perceived needs and are not integrated into the normal structures and activities of ministries. Given the need for such integration, the cost of the activities, and problems in recruiting personnel with the required competence to carry them out, the urgent need for rationalization is clear.

All national assessment activities in Africa share a number of features. In theory, all are designed to provide information for policymaking. (While this was not true of the *Programme d'Analyse des Systèmes Educatifs des Pays de la CONFEMEN* [PASEC] in its early stages, when it was perceived primarily as a research/technical activity, ministry officials in time became interested and involved.) All the assessments view capacity building and the strengthening of the policymaker/researcher nexus as major objectives. In all the assessments, pupil achievements are assessed in a sample of schools in basic curriculum areas and background information is collected from teachers and students. These data are then related to the pupils' achievements in an attempt to identify the factors associated with achievement. (Although it should be noted that there are departures from this general pattern; for example, in some studies, teachers also have taken tests.)

The input–output model on which national assessments are based, following the tradition of the original international studies of achievement (see Husén and Postlethwaite 1996), may have led to a tendency to accord the research function of assessments (for example, to help identify or "understand" the causes of achievement) a higher status than its management function (for example, to provide immediate feedback to decision-makers about the condition of the education system). It may also have led to a tendency to interpret associations between input factors and student outcomes in terms of cause and effect. This can result in unwarranted, and possibly incorrect, conclusions for at least three reasons:

- causality cannot normally be inferred from data that are all collected at the same time, as is the case in a national assessment;
- the instruments used to collect background information, and the way variables are constructed for analysis, may not identify those aspects of the environment that are most important to achievement (such as the "cultural" and "social" capital of the home and community); and
- the type of statistical analysis (for example, hierarchical linear modeling) required to explore relationships is likely to be unfamiliar to many of the personnel involved in national assessments.

For these reasons, it would seem more appropriate that the data obtained in a national assessment be considered primarily as a tool of strategic management in the context of educational planning (Verspoor 1992). Under this approach, assessment results would be interpreted and used in a "managerial" context, providing evidence for decisions (such as the type of in-service needed). The more complex exploration of "causes" of achievement would be left to traditional research.

There is some evidence that the findings of national assessments have made their way into government deliberations, reviews, and documents, but the extent to which they have been used in managerial decisions is unclear. We may assume that such use is most likely where senior policy-makers and managers have contributed to the initiation of a national assessment and to the questions that the assessment was designed to address. There is less evidence that the information from national assessments has affected school practice, but this is not surprising. National assessments have not been in existence for long, and one would expect that it would take some time before they have an impact. Furthermore, using results to affect school practice is not easy; the effort to achieve this has been made in several countries, but its impact has not been assessed.

When considering the role of national assessments, it is important to bear in mind that their successful execution requires a considerable degree of technical competence. The development of the capacity to achieve this competence is essential if the information the assessments generate is to be valid, reliable, and thus capable of underpinning the decisions of policymakers and managers. This in turn requires that governments and donors be prepared to provide the financial support to put in place the appropriate design, instrumentation, sampling, and analysis capability.

Few African countries have participated in the international assessments of student achievement that have been designed for industrialized countries. Some of the national assessments that have been carried out in Africa also permit international comparisons to be made, however, and there are indications that some countries are interested in developing this capacity further. This said, the main value in international collaboration would seem to reside in the opportunities it provides for the pooling of resources to develop the skills required to carry out national-level assessments.

Because they are integral to teaching and learning, teachers' assessment practices in the classroom would seem to have the greatest potential to enhance students' achievements. However, these assessment practices often are of poor quality and are unlikely to foster the development of higher-order and problem-solving competencies in students. Unfortunately, improving teachers' assessment practices also is more difficult and expensive than improving or developing other forms of assessment. It involves, for example, (a) improving the assessment skills of teachers (to be achieved through preservice and in-service courses that take account of the conditions, including class size and the availability of resources, under which teachers work); (b) providing guidance to teachers in the use of assessment information in making decisions regarding grade promotions; (c) providing examples (at the end of chapters in textbooks) of good assessment practices; (d) developing ways of communicating information on assessment reforms to classroom teachers and of providing assistance to teachers in interpreting the significance of this information for classroom practice. It is particularly important that the many teachers who have been hastily hired to meet the EFA agenda are provided with training in classroom assessment.

One conclusion of the review presented in this paper is that while assessment information can improve policy and the management of resources in education and can shape teachers' instructional practices, success is not assured. Success in the first place is dependent on the political will of government to support the collection and use of assessment data. This support is required at two levels. At one level, national assessment systems should be institutionalized and integrated into the structures and processes of government policy formulation and decision-making. This requires the integration of information from assessments into Educational Management Information Systems, and the establishment of procedures that can ensure that the information is provided to all those persons and groups involved in policy and management. In developing the capacity to achieve these objectives, countries will be able to draw on the assistance of the National Education Statistical Information Systems (NESIS), a program initiated by the Working Group on Education Statistics (WGES) of the Association for the Development of Education in Africa (ADEA). (To date, 47 countries have participated in NESIS activities.) It also is important that national assessments be aligned with other aspects of the education system, including other assessment systems (including the alignment of standards), curricula, teacher education, school capacity building, and measures to address inequities.

Action will also be required at the school level. Adequate channels of communication first and foremost will be required to inform teachers of changes. When intervention involves primarily the provision of space or materials, it may be direct and relatively straightforward. It is less likely to be so when problems relate to instructional objectives, equity, and quality (Verspoor 1989, 1992), in which case teachers may need considerable and continuing support to interpret reforms and to devise appropriate teaching strategies. Inspectors, supervisors, and principal teachers, all of whom may require training, have a role to play in providing this support.

There are a number of implications related to the differences between the kinds of assessments that are available for use, and these implications should be borne in mind when considering the role that the assessments might play in improving the quality of education. First, the use of public examinations and classroom assessment as vehicles of reform primarily will involve the modification of existing practices. The use of national and international assessments, in contrast, will require new procedures. Second, the likelihood of assessment influencing the learning environment of the classroom and the achievements of individual students is higher in the case of public examinations and classroom assessment than in the case of national and international assessments, since the influence of the latter is more remote and would need to be mediated through policy and managerial decisions. Third, classroom assessment differs from the other forms in that it is essentially "private." Information derived from classroom assessment becomes public when it is conveyed to parents or where it contributes to the grade awarded in a public examination, but most of it remains within the walls of the classroom. Finally, while classroom assessment may have the greatest potential to influence student achievements, it also is the most difficult for an outside agency to alter.

In conclusion, we should note the comments of observers of education in Africa that past reforms have not worked very well. Certainly, it seems true that single-focus, isolated efforts usually have failed to fulfill their promise. Would proposals to use assessment to improve the quality of education fare any better? If assessment reforms are not integrated into the structures and processes of government policy and decision-making, and if they are not aligned with other major instructional guidance systems, the answer would seem to be no. If, on the other hand, they are, there are grounds for optimism.

There are also other grounds for optimism, despite the many difficulties that face education in Africa that were outlined in the early part of this paper. Following Dakar, the formulation of the Millennium Development Goals (MDGs), and the emphasis on national Poverty Reduction Strategy Papers (PRSPs), policies, implementation plans, and activities have been and are being designed to instill a sense of urgency and to create a climate of accountability. Furthermore, assessment reform should provide objective information for decision-making that has not been available in the past. Assessment reform efforts will also benefit from the commitment among Association for the Development of Education in Africa (ADEA) partners to the development of a "culture" of finding solutions and policy responses within the African context (ADEA 1999). If these conditions are realized, an important role can be envisaged for assessment in enhancing the quality of student learning.

Recommendations

The following recommendations are proposed for the consideration of ministries of education and other relevant education authorities and stakeholders.

- On the basis that assessment systems should be designed to be mutually supportive in improving the quality of student learning, the ministry of education, in collaboration with stakeholders, should develop overall policies for assessment in which the goals of public examination, national assessment, and classroom assessment are aligned.
- Assessment policies should be sensitive to and supportive of policies governing other components of the education system, including teacher education, school capacity building, and measures to address inequities, to provide systemic, multifaceted, and coherent approaches to improving student learning.
- The information derived from assessments should be integrated into policy and decision-making structures of the ministry of education to serve as an input to education planning and strategic management, and should also be conveyed to those responsible for curricula and textbooks.
- School curricula and public examinations should be reviewed to determine their relevance to the everyday lives of students and the needs of the economy, and appropriate adjustments made. The review should have in mind the goals of Education For All.
- Efforts to reform public examinations, to improve curriculum coverage and the quality of student learning, should continue.
- Public examinations should be reviewed to ensure that their content and difficulty level reflect their certification function. If necessary, adjustments should be made.
- The scope of public examinations should be broadened, and the certificates awarded to students should include data on aspects of student development not assessed in the written terminal examination.
- National assessments should be a response to the information needs of the ministry of education and other stakeholders. Activities should be rationalized in countries in which more than one system operates.
- The ministry of education should seek to achieve high technical standards in national assessments by ensuring that the technical means and organizational capacity to monitor student achievements are developed.
- In recognition of the central role of teachers in improving the quality of student learning, steps should be taken to:
  (a) improve the assessment skills of teachers (through preservice and in-service courses that give adequate regard to the conditions, including class size and the availability of resources, under which teachers work);
  (b) provide guidance in the use of assessment information when making decisions regarding grade promotions;
  (c) provide examples of good assessment practices at the end of chapters in textbooks; and

(d) develop ways of communicating information on assessment and reforms to classroom teachers, and provide assistance in interpreting the significance of this information for classroom practice.

- Work should be undertaken to establish equivalences between achievements and qualifications awarded in the formal and nonformal sectors of the education system.

References

Ackers, J., J. Migoli, and J. Nzomo. 2001. "Identifying and Addressing the Causes of Declining Participation Rates in Kenyan Primary Schools." *International Journal of Educational Development* 21:361–374.

ADEA (Association for the Development of Education in Africa). 1999. *What Works and What's New in Education: Africa Speaks.* Paris: ADEA.

———. 2002. *Reaching Out, Reaching All. Sustaining Effective Policy and Practice for Education in Africa. Fighting HIV/AIDS.* Proceedings of the ADEA Biennial Meeting, Arusha, Tanzania, October 7–11, 2001. Paris: ADEA.

Airasian, P. W. 1988. "Measurement-Driven Instruction: A Closer Look." *Educational Measurement: Issues and Practice* 7(4):6–11.

Arnott, A., and Z. Kubeka. 1997. *Mathematics and Science Teachers. Demand, Utilization, Supply and Training in South Africa.* Johannesburg: Edusource.

Bamgbose, A. 1991. *Language and the Nation: The Language Question in Sub-Saharan Africa.* Edinburgh: Edinburgh University Press.

Beaton, A. E., T. N. Postlethwaite, K. N. Ross, D. Spearritt, and R. M. Wolf. 1999. *The Benefits and Limitations of International Achievement Studies.* Paris: UNESCO (United Nations Educational, Scientific and Cultural Organization) International Institute for Educational Planning; International Academy of Education.

Black, P., and D. Wiliam. 1998. "Assessment and Classroom Learning." *Assessment in Education* 5:7–74.

Bude, U. 1993. "Strategies for Using Information to Improve Learning Conditions and Instructional Practices at the School Level." In D. W. Chapman and L. O. Mählck, eds., *From Data to Action: Information Systems in Educational Planning.* Paris: UNESCO (United Nations Educational, Scientific and Cultural Organization) International Institute for Educational Planning.

———. 1997. "End of Primary School Examination in Eastern and Southern Africa: An Overview." In U. Bude and K. Lewin, eds., *Improving Test Design.* Vol. 2: *Assessment of Science and Agriculture in Primary Schools in Africa; Twelve Country Cases Reviewed.* Bonn: Education, Science and Documentation Centre.

Bude, U., and K. Lewin. 1997. "Introduction." In U. Bude and K. Lewin, eds., *Improving Test Design.* Vol. 1: *Constructing Test Instruments, Analysing Results and Improving Assessment Quality in Primary Schools in Africa.* Bonn: Education, Science and Documentation Centre.

Buly, M. R., and S. W. Valencia. 2002. "Below the Bar: Profiles of Students Who Fail State Reading Assessments." *Educational Evaluation and Policy Analysis* 24:219–239.

Burnstein, L., ed. 1993. *The IEA Study of Mathematics III: Student Growth and Classroom Processes.* Oxford: Pergamon.

Carron, G., and T. N. Châu. 1996. *The Quality of Primary Schools in Different Development Contexts.* Paris: UNESCO (United Nations Educational, Scientific and Cultural Organization) Publishing/International Institute for Educational Planning.

Chapman, D. W., and L. O. Mählck. 1993. "Improving Educational Quality through Better Use of Information." In D. W. Chapman and L. O. Mählck, eds., *From Data to Action: Information Systems in Educational Planning.* Paris: UNESCO (United Nations Educational, Scientific and Cultural Organization): International Institute for Educational Planning.

Chapman, D. W., and C. W. Snyder. 2000. "Can High Stakes National Testing Improve Instruction? Reexamining Conventional Wisdom." *International Journal of Educational Development* 20:457–474.

Chinapah, V. 1997. *Handbook on Monitoring Learning Achievement: Towards Capacity Building.* Paris: UNESCO (United Nations Educational, Scientific and Cultural Organization).

Chinapah, V., E. M. H'ddigui, A. Kanji, W. Falayajo, C. O. Fomba, O. Hamissou, A. Rafalimanana, and A. Byamugisha. 2000. *With Africa for Africa: Towards Quality Education for All.* Pretoria: Human Sciences Research Council.

Cizek, G. J. 2001. *Setting Performance Standards: Concepts, Methods, and Perspectives.* Mahwah, N.J.: Lawrence Erlbaum.

Clayton, T. 1998. "Explanations for the Use of Languages of Wider Communication in Education in Developing Countries." *International Journal of Educational Development* 18:145–157.

Eisemon, T. O. 1990. "Examination Policies to Strengthen Primary Schooling in African Countries." *International Journal of Educational Development* 10:69–82.

———. 1997. *Reducing Repetition: Issues and Strategies.* Paris: UNESCO (United Nations Educational, Scientific and Cultural Organization) International Institute for Educational Planning.

Eisemon, T. O., V. L. Patel, and J. Abagi. 1987. "Read These Instructions Carefully: Examination Reform and Improving Health Education in Kenya." *International Journal of Educational Development* 8:55–66.

Eisemon, T. O., J. Schwille, R. Prouty, F. Ukobizoba, D. Kana, and G. Manirabona. 1993. "Providing Quality Education when Resources Are Scarce: Strategies for Increasing Primary School Effectiveness in Burundi." In H. M. Levin and M. E. Lockheed, eds., *Effective Schools in Developing Countries*. London: Falmer Press.

ERGESE (Evaluative Research of the General Education System in Ethiopia). 1986. *A Quality Study: Summary Report Presented to the Executive Committee of ERGESE*. Addis Ababa: ERGESE.

Eritrea Department of General Education. 1999. *Competence Test Report 1998/99*. Asmara: Eritrea Department of General Education.

Grant, S., P. Peterson, and A. Shojgreen-Downer. 1996. "Learning to Teach Mathematics in the Context of System Reform." *American Educational Research Journal* 33:500–543.

Greaney, V., and T. Kellaghan. 1996a. *Monitoring the Learning Outcomes of Education Systems*. Washington, D.C.: World Bank.

———. 1996b. "The Integrity of Public Examinations in Developing Countries." In H. Goldstein and T. Lewis, eds., *Assessment: Problems, Developments and Statistical Issues*. New York: Wiley.

Grisay, A., and L. Mählck. 1991. *The Quality of Education in Developing Countries: A Review of Some Research Studies and Policy Documents*. Paris: International Institute for Educational Planning.

Heyneman, S. P. 1988. "Improving University Selection, Educational Research, and Educational Management in Developing Countries: The Role of Examinations and Standardized Testing." In S. Heyneman and I. Fägerlind, eds., *University Examinations and Standardized Testing*. Washington, D.C.: World Bank.

Heyneman, S. P., and A. W. Ransom. 1992. "Using Examinations and Testing to Improve Educational Quality." In M. A. Eckstein and H. J. Noah, eds., *Examinations: Comparative and International Studies*. Oxford: Pergamon.

Himmel, E. 1996. "National Assessment in Chile." In P. Murphy, V. Greaney, M. E. Lockheed, and C. Rojas, eds., *National Assessments: Testing the System*. Washington, D.C.: World Bank.

Howie, S. J. 1999. "National Assessment in an International Context: Building Capacity and Expertise in South Africa." Paper presented at World Bank Conference on Human Development, 3–5 March 1999, Washington, D.C.

———. 2001. *Mathematics and Science Programmes in Grade 8 in South Africa 1989/99. TIMSS-R South Africa*. Pretoria: Human Sciences Research Council.

———. 2002. *English Language Proficiency and Contextual Factors Influencing Mathematics Achievement of Secondary School Pupils in South Africa*. Ph.D. dissertation, University of Twente.

Husén, T., and T. N. Postlethwaite. 1996. "A Brief History of the International Association for the Evaluation of Educational Achievement (IEA)." *Assessment in Education* 3:129–141.

Kanjee, A. 2003. "Using Assessment Resource Banks to Improve the Teaching and Learning Process." In *Improving the Quality of Primary Education: Good Practices and Emerging Models of District Development*. Pretoria: District Development Support Programme/Research Triangle Institute.

Kellaghan, T. 1992. "Examination Systems in Africa: Between Internationalization and Indigenization." In M. A. Eckstein and H. J. Noah, eds., *Examinations: Comparative and International Studies*. Oxford: Pergamon.

———. 1996a. "Can Public Examinations Be Used to Provide Information for National Assessment?" In P. Murphy, V. Greaney, M. E. Lockheed, and C. Rojas, eds., *National Assessments: Testing the System*. Washington, D.C.: World Bank.

———. 1996b. "IEA Studies and Educational Policy." *Assessment in Education* 3:143–160.

———. 2002. *Assessment in the Swazi System of Education*. Dublin: Educational Research Centre.

———. 2003. "Local, National, and International Levels of System Evaluation: Introduction." In T. Kellaghan and D. L. Stufflebeam, eds., *International Handbook of Educational Evaluation*. Dordrecht: Kluwer Academic.

Kellaghan, T., and E. Farrell. 1998. "A Study of the Feasibility of Obtaining, and the Utility for Describing Learning Outcomes of Data Relating to Public Examination Performance at the End of Primary Schooling." Unpublished report submitted to the United Nations Educational, Scientific and Cultural Organization on behalf of the International Association for Educational Assessment.

Kellaghan, T., and V. Greaney. 1992. *Using Examinations to Improve Education: A Study in Fourteen African Countries*. Washington, D.C.: World Bank.

———. 2001a. "The Globalisation of Assessment in the 20th Century." *Assessment in Education* 8:87–102.

———. 2001b. *Using Assessment to Improve the Quality of Education*. Paris: UNESCO (United Nations Educational, Scientific and Cultural Organization) International Institute for Educational Planning.

Kellaghan, T., and G. F. Madaus. 2000. "Outcome Evaluation." In D. L. Stufflebeam, G. F. Madaus, and T. Kellaghan, eds., *Evaluation Models: Viewpoints on Educational and Human Services Evaluation* (second edition). Boston: Kluwer Academic.

Kellaghan, T., G. F. Madaus, and A. Raczek. 1996. *The Use of External Examinations to Improve Student Motivation*. Washington, D.C.: American Educational Research Association.

Kelly, M. J. 1991. *Education in a Declining Economy: The Case of Zambia, 1975–1985.* Washington D.C.: World Bank.

Kudjoh, A., and A. Mingat. 1993. "Toward a Better Understanding of the Functioning of School Systems for Better Decision-Making: The Case of Primary Schools in Togo." In D. W. Chapman and L. O. Mählck, eds., *From Data to Action: Information Systems in Educational Planning.* Paris: UNESCO (United Nations Educational, Scientific and Cultural Organization) International Institute for Educational Planning.

Kulpoo, D., and P. Coustère. 1999. "Developing National Capacities for Assessment and Monitoring through Effective Partnerships." In *Partnerships for Capacity Building and Quality Improvements in Education: Papers from the ADEA 1997 Biennial Meeting, Dakar, Senegal.* Paris: ADEA (Association for the Development of Education in Africa).

Kyalo, F. K. 1997. "The Use of Examination Results for Monitoring Performance of Schools, Districts and Provinces." In U. Bude and K. Lewin, eds., *Improving Test Design.* Volume 1: *Constructing Test Instruments, Analysing Results and Improving Assessment Quality in Primary Schools in Africa.* Bonn: Education, Science and Documentation Centre.

Le Mahieu, P. G. 1984. "The Effects on Achievement and Instructional Content of a Program of Student Monitoring through Frequent Testing." *Educational Evaluation and Policy Analysis* 6:175–187.

Le Mahieu, P. G., and G. Leinhardt. 1985. "Overlap: Influencing What's Taught. A Process Model of Teachers' Content Selection." *Journal of Classroom Interaction* 21(1):2–11.

Lewin, K., and M. Dunne. 2000. "Policy and Practice in Assessment in Anglophone Africa: Does Globalisation Explain Convergence?" *Assessment in Education* 7:379–399.

Linn, R. L. 1983. "Testing and Instruction: Links and Distinctions." *Journal of Educational Measurement* 20:179–189.

———. 2000. "Assessments and Accountability." *Educational Research* 29(2):4–16.

Little, A. 1982. "The Role of Examinations in the Promotion of the 'Paper Qualification Syndrome.'" In *Paper Qualifications Syndrome (PQS) and Unemployment of School Leavers: A Comparative Sub-Regional Study.* Addis Ababa: International Labour Office.

London, N. A. 1997. "A National Strategy for Systems-Wide Curriculum Improvement in Trinidad and Tobago." In D. W. Chapman, L. O. Mählck, and A. E. M. Smulders, eds., *From Planning to Action: Government Initiatives for Improving School-Level Practice.* Paris: International Institute for Educational Planning; Oxford: Pergamon.

Machingaidze, T., P. Pfukani, and S. Shumba. (n.d.) *The Quality of Education: Some Policy Suggestions Based on a Survey of Schools, Zimbabwe.* Paris:

International Institute for Educational Planning; Harare: Ministry of Education and Culture.

Madaus, G. F. 1988. "The Influence of Testing on the Curriculum." In L. N. Tanner, ed., *Critical Issues in Curriculum. Eighty-Seventh Yearbook of the National Society for the Study of Education*. Chicago: University of Chicago Press.

Madaus, G. F., and V. Greaney. 1985. "The Irish Experience in Competency Testing: Implications for American Education." *American Journal of Education* 93:268–294.

Madaus, G. F., and T. Kellaghan. 1992. "Curriculum Evaluation and Assessment." In P. W. Jackson, ed., *Handbook of Research on Curriculum*. New York: Macmillan.

Marope, P. T. M. 1999. "Capacity Development through ADEA Working Groups: Applicable Practices and Lessons. In *Partnerships for Capacity Building and Quality Improvements in Education. Papers from the ADEA 1997 Biennial Meeting, Dakar, Senegal*. Paris: Association for the Development of Education in Africa.

Mazibuko, E. Z., and R. Magagula. 2003. "Quality of Education in Sub-Saharan Africa: A Literature Review with Specific Reference to Swaziland c. 1991–2001." Unpublished review financed by the Association for the Development of Education in Africa (ADEA) through the Educational Network in Eastern and Southern Africa (ERNESA).

Mioko, S. 1998. *Gender versus Socioeconomic Status and School Location Differences in Grade 6 Reading Literacy in Five African Countries*. Harare: Ministry of Education and Culture.

Mislevy, R. J. 1995. "What Can We Learn from International Assessments?" *Educational Evaluation and Policy Analysis* 17:419–437.

Namibia Ministry of Education and Culture, Florida State University, and Harvard University. 1994. *How Much Do Namibia's Children Learn in School? Findings from the 1992 National Learner Baseline Assessment*. Windhoek: Ministry of Education and Culture.

Naumann, J., and P. Wolf. 2001. "The Performance of African Primary Education Systems: Critique and New Analysis of PASEC Data for Senegal." *Prospects* 31:373–391.

N'tchougan-Sonou, C. 2001. "Automatic Promotion or Large-Scale Repetition: Which Way to Quality?" *International Journal of Educational Development* 21:149–162.

Ogundare, S. 1988. "Curriculum Development: A Description of the Development of the National Curriculum for Primary Social Studies in Nigeria." *Educational Studies* 14:43–50.

Omolewa, M., and T. Kellaghan. 2003. "Educational Evaluation in Africa." In T. Kellaghan and D. L. Stufflebeam, eds., *International Handbook of Educational Evaluation*. Dordrecht: Kluwer Academic.

O-saki, K. M., and A. O. Agu. 2002. "A Study of Classroom Interaction in Primary Schools in the United Republic of Tanzania." *Prospects* 32:103–116.

Ouane, A., ed. 2003. *Towards a Multilingual Culture of Education*. Paris: UNESCO (United Nations Educational, Scientific and Cultural Organization) International Institute for Educational Planning.

Oxenham, J. 1983. "What Examinations Test and Emphasize: An Analysis of the Lesotho Primary and Junior Secondary Examinations." In *The Education Sector Survey. Annexes to the Report of the Task Force*. Maseru: Government of Lesotho.

Pennycuick, D. 1990a. "Factors Influencing the Introduction of Continuous Assessment Systems in Developing Countries." In D. Layton, ed., *Innovations in Science and Technology Education*. Volume 3. Paris: UNESCO (United Nations Educational, Scientific and Cultural Organization).

————. 1990b. "The Introduction of Continuous Assessment Systems at Secondary Level in Developing Countries." In P. Broadfoot, R. Murphy, and H. Torrance, eds., *Changing Educational Assessment: International Perspectives and Trends*. London: Routledge.

Popham, W. J. 1983. "Measurement as an Instructional Catalyst." *New Directions for Testing and Measurement* 17:19–30.

————. 1987. "The Merits of Measurement-Driven Instruction." *Phi Delta Kappan* 68:679–682.

Postlethwaite, T. N., and D. E Wiley. 1992. *The IEA Study of Science II: Science Achievement in Twenty-Three Countries*. Oxford: Pergamon.

Rharade, A. 1997. "Educational Reform in Kenya." *Prospects* 27:163–179.

Rollnick, M., S. Manyatsi, F. Lubben, and J. Bradley. 1998. "A Model for Studying Gaps in Education: A Swaziland Case Study in the Learning of Science." *International Journal of Educational Development* 18:453–465.

Romberg, T. A. 1999. "The Impact of International Comparisons on National Policy." In G. Kaiser, E. Luna, and I. Huntley, eds., *International Comparisons in Mathematics Education*. London: Falmer.

Ross, K. N., P. Pfukani, J. Nzomo, D. Makuwa, S. Nassur, J. Kanyika, T. Machingaidze, G. Milner, D. Kulpoo, T. N. Postlethwaite, M. Saito, and S. Leite 2000. *Translating Educational Assessment Findings into Educational Policy and Reform Measures: Lessons from the SACMEQ Initiative in Africa*. Paris: UNESCO (United Nations Educational, Scientific and Cultural Organization).

Samoff, J. 1999. "Cooperation, but Limited Control and Little Ownership." In *Partnerships for Capacity Building and Quality Improvements in Education. Papers from the ADEA Biennial Meeting, Dakar, Senegal*. Paris: Association for the Development of Education in Africa.

Schiefelbein, E. 1993. "The Use of National Assessments to Improve Primary Education in Chile." In D. W. Chapman and L. O. Mählck, eds., *From*

Data to Action: Information Systems in Educational Planning. Paris: UNESCO (United Nations Educational, Scientific and Cultural Organization) International Institute for Educational Planning; Oxford: Pergamon.

Snyder, C. W., B. Prince, G. Lohanson, C. Odaet, L. Jaji, and M. Beatty. 1997. *Exam Fervor and Fever: Case Studies of the Influence of Primary Leaving Examinations on Uganda Classrooms, Teachers, and Pupils.* Washington, D.C.: Academy for Educational Development.

Somerset, A. 1987. *Examination Reform in Kenya.* Washington, D.C.: World Bank.

———. 1988. "Examinations as an Instrument to Improve Pedagogy." In S. P. Heynemann and I. Fägerlind, eds., *University Examinations and Standardized Testing: Principles, Experience, and Policy Options.* Washington, D.C.: World Bank.

———. 1996. "Examinations and Educational Quality." In A. Little and A. Wolf, eds., *Assessment in Transition: Learning, Monitoring and Selection in International Perspective.* Oxford: Pergamon.

Takala, T. 1998. "Making Educational Policy under the Influence of External Assistance and National Politics: A Comparative Analysis of the Education Sector Policy Documents of Ethiopia, Mozambique, Namibia and Zambia." *International Journal of Educational Development* 18:319–335.

Torrance, H. 1997. "Assessment, Accountability, and Standards: Using Assessment to Control the Reform of Schooling." In A. H. Halsey, H. Lauder, P. Brown, and A. S. Wells, eds., *Education: Culture, Economy, and Society.* Oxford: Oxford University Press.

U.K. (United Kingdom) Department of Education and Science and Welsh Office. 1988. *Task Group on Assessment and Testing: A Report.* London: Her Majesty's Stationery Office.

UNESCO (United Nations Educational, Scientific and Cultural Organization). 1990. *World Declaration on Education for All: Meeting Basic Learning Needs.* New York: UNESCO.

———. 2000a. *The Dakar Framework for Action. Education for All: Meeting Our Collective Commitments.* Paris: UNESCO.

———. 2000b. *Education for All: Status and Trends 2000. Assessing Learning Achievement 2000.* Paris: UNESCO.

———. 2002. *Education for All: Is the World on Track? EFA Global Monitoring Report.* Paris: UNESCO.

———. 2003a. *Monitoring Learning Achievement (MLA) Project: Update.* Paris: UNESCO.

———. 2003b. Southern African Consortium for Monitoring Educational Quality (SACMEQ). Harare: UNESCO.

V dMerwe, I. F. J. 1999. *Case Study on the Establishment of a National Examinations and Assessment System for School Examinations in Namibia.* Windhoek: Ministry of Basic Education and Culture.

Verspoor, A. 1989. *Pathways to Change: Improving the Quality of Education in Developing Countries*. Washington, D.C.: World Bank.

————. 1992. *Challenges to the Planning of Education*. Washington, D.C.: World Bank.

Wasanga, P. M. 1997. "Testing and Monitoring Procedures Developed for Primary Schools." In U. Bude and K. Lewin, eds., *Improving Test Design. Volume 1: Constructing Test Instruments, Analysing Results and Improving Assessment Quality in Primary Schools in Africa*. Bonn: Education, Science and Documentation Centre.

World Bank. 1988. *Education in Sub-Saharan Africa: Policies for Adjustment, Revitalization, and Expansion*. Washington, D.C.: World Bank.

World Conference on Education for All. 1990. *World Declaration on Education for All*. Adopted by the World Conference on Education for All: Meeting Basic Learning Needs. New York: UNDP/UNESCO/UNICEF/World Bank (United Nations Development Programme/United Nations Educational, Scientific and Cultural Organization /United Nations Children's Fund /World Bank).

Index